Men, War
and Film

Men, War and Film

The *Calling Blighty*
Films of
World War II

Steve Hawley

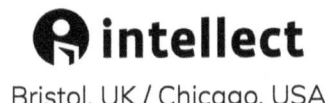

Bristol, UK / Chicago, USA

First published in the UK in 2022 by
Intellect, The Mill, Parnall Road, Fishponds, Bristol, BS16 3JG, UK

First published in the USA in 2022 by
Intellect, The University of Chicago Press, 1427 E. 60th Street,
Chicago, IL 60637, USA

A catalogue record for this book is available from
the British Library.

Copy editor: MPS Limited
Cover designer: Aleksandra Szumlas
Cover image: Director Captain Hamilton-Webb with unnamed
Indian cameraman and assistant Dennis Davies,
of the *Calling Blighty* film unit, Burma 1945. © IWM
Production manager: Debora Nicosia
Typesetter: MPS Limited

Print ISBN 978-1-78938-511-3
ePDF ISBN 978-1-78938-513-7
ePUB ISBN 978-1-78938-512-0

To find out about all our publications, please visit our website.
There you can subscribe to our e-newsletter, browse or download our current
catalogue and buy any titles that are in print.

www.intellectbooks.com

This is a peer-reviewed publication.

To Marion Hewitt, Director of the North West Film Archive,
for her unfailing support.

Contents

Figures

Introduction:
Talking with the Dead

The past is not fixed in the way that linear time suggests. We can return. We can pick up what we dropped. We can mend what others broke. We can talk with the dead.

(Jeanette Winterson, *Why Be Happy When You Could Be Normal?* 2009: 58)

Blighty, an informal term for Britain or England, used by soldiers of the First and Second World Wars. First used by soldiers in the Indian army, Anglo-Indian alteration of Urdu bilāyatī, wilāyatī 'foreign'.

(*Lexico* 2020)

In September 1943, an expectant audience of wives, mothers, sweethearts and children gathered in the evening at the Curzon cinema in London's Mayfair, for what was to be a unique event. Five thousand miles away, their sons and husbands serving in one of the most arduous and alien conflicts of World War II had been gathered in a studio resembling a NAAFI canteen, to deliver filmed messages to their families at home in London. The men may have been overawed and a little stilted but the reaction in the cinema was an overwhelming combination of tears mixed with laughter. 'I suppose if you put all the cinemas in London together, the pleasure they provided would come nowhere near the happiness this ten-minute film gave' (*Liverpool Daily Post* 1943: 2). A year later the *Calling Blighty* film scheme had been extended to all regions of the United Kingdom. 'I'd better say a few words now that I'm here; it was six years ago we last spoke, do you remember?' (*CB* 241 1946). Louis Shimberg was speaking to his family in Manchester, from an army camp in Burma over 75 years ago, looking directly into the film camera, at his wife and children as he imagined them in the cinema in Britain ('Blighty'). There is something extraordinary and compelling about his message and those of the 1200 of the servicemen (and a very few women) that still exist. They seem to shrink time, to channel the words of our grandfathers and great-grandfathers into our present and to make the past visible.

The *Calling Blighty* films of World War II are remarkable documents, which are at once filmed postcards, a window on the authentic voices of ordinary men engaged in what even in 1944 was a distant and forgotten war against a Japanese invader, and also instruments of remembrance, memorials just as much as inscriptions and chiseled stones. They were filmed by the Combined Kinematograph Services (CKS) between 1943 and 1946 in India and Burma to improve the morale of men engaged in the war against the Japanese, waged in order to retake the then British empire colony of Burma, now Myanmar. Uncertain how to present themselves on screen, their only experience of cinema a fantasy world of escape, the men try to find their own voices, and many were able to overcome the unfamiliar experience and distil their thoughts into reassuring messages of love. Even when what was actually said was prosaic, their direct gaze into the camera to their families, blown up to cinema screen size is as powerfully evocative today as it must have been then. The men were grouped together according to their town or city, and the subsequent films screened in regional cinemas in Sheffield, Worcester, Brighton and across the United Kingdom to audiences of mothers, wives, sweethearts and other family members. The aim was to connect men of the Fourteenth

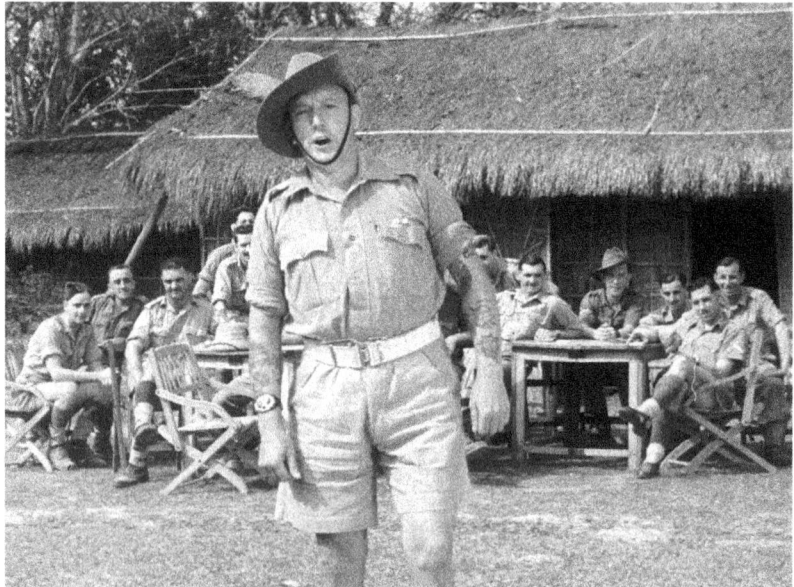

FIGURE I.1: Sgt Major Stan Walker singing Ilkla Moor Baht 'at (*CB* 1945). © Yorkshire Film Archive.

Army (the 'Forgotten Army') with their loved ones back home, in an era of slow and censored mail, and the impossibility of home leave due to the vast distances involved, but the effect was to reinforce a sense of place, the identity of regional communities across the United Kingdom.

Men from Sheffield would send greetings and remember their local football team Sheffield Wednesday ('If you're down at Owlerton, give a shout to Jackie Robinson from me' [*CB 252 1946*]), and holidays at Mablethorpe, all spoken in their local accent. At the end of one film, Stan Walker led South Yorkshire men singing together the Yorkshire anthem, On Ilkley Moor Baht 'at, and this regional identity was often expressed in communal song: 'She's a Lassie from Lancashire', for the Manchester men, or 'Sailing up the Clyde' for the men from Glasgow. In fact, almost for the first time, the working-class man can be seen onscreen speaking in a regional accent, at a time when wartime film was dominated by the clipped tones of the upper middle officer class. In one of the most popular wartime films, albeit a Hollywood version of buttoned up British reserve, *Mrs Miniver* (1942), Greer Garson as the eponymous heroine is middle-class, a Londoner and her uncomplaining patriotism struck a chord with many filmgoers, especially women. 'You can sit at the Empire (in Leicester Square) and hear practically the whole house weeping' (Farmer: 217). But Wilf Parker's voice from Sheffield speaking to his brother Harry about the Owls football club, and the hundreds of other voices in the *Calling Blighty* films are a world away from this. They speak with authenticity, rooted in their communities that seldom then appeared on screen, and they address their families in the same communities, with local shorthand references, the Regent Cinema House and their local football team, far removed from the dominant cinematic picture presented in well-meaning films such as *Millions Like Us* (1943) or *In Which We Serve* (1942). The latter film, whilst praised, was noted even at the time as reinforcing class relationships and presenting an apparently fixed and settled view of British community (Aldgate and Richards 1986: 209).

In terms of what they say, these voices from a distant war are highly constrained, partly by wartime military censorship, partly by the need to reassure families who were desperate for reassurance and also by the conventions of the written form that the men unconsciously adopted. That the messages were often more like spoken postcards – 'Hello Evelyn, I hope you find this as it leaves me' (*CB 252 1946*), should not surprise us, nor the frequent focus on mail received (or not). A reliance on written letters from home has been the soldier's lifeline for centuries until very recently and the development of smartphones and the internet. The men were also trying to find out how they should present themselves on film at the same time as they were inhibited by the codes of masculine expression of a past era. However, the circumscribed form of speech that the men and women assume is thrown into high relief by our present knowledge of the terrible war they were engaged in. It was one where the conditions of combat were unimaginable to a home audience, affected as the service personnel were by disease, heat, the monsoon, poor food and a feared and ruthless enemy, the Japanese. Sometimes men make reference to this unintelligible gulf between their on-screen appearance, the sun shining, the exotic jungle and the reality. 'When you see this stuff behind us [gestures at a Burmese river] don't think we're at Blackpool. We're not; far from it' (*CB* 212 1945). But most are silent about the horrors they endured, a silence that almost always stretched throughout the rest of their lives. There is a strange dislocation between the horrors of the unseen war and the often cheerful demeanour of the men who speak perkily of keeping their chins up, being in the pink and telling us to keep smiling, and this paradoxically deepens the power of the images, with our present-day hindsight of the reality that they were enduring.

The *Calling Blighty* films, almost eighty hours of them over the three years they were produced, can take their place amongst the wartime output of fiction, newsreel and documentary film. Although not documentary, and often not on general release but screened just to family and friends of the servicemen – however, these were crowded screenings of several hundred a time, and sometimes repeated – these are filmed documents and can be compared with the depiction of working-class men at the time in British documentary film. In terms of sheer volume, the films are significant as a part of wartime output – there were 391 films produced overall, each about 12 minutes long, and an impressive 60 still survive, divided between various national and regional film archives. Of these, 23 alone are of the Manchester area, a rare and lucky find in the basement of Manchester Town Hall during renovations, and more are from towns nearby and the greater North-West.

The depiction of men from all strata of society and from all regions of the United Kingdom in an unscripted naturalistic context was highly limited at that time within film of any kind. These are the first such filmed messages in the world in such a large concentration and covering such a broad range of men from across a single nation. Apart from rare newsreel footage and simultaneous but much smaller *Calling Blighty* initiatives had been created by commercial companies such as Pathé, as we will see, the predominantly upper-middle-class documentary makers of the 1930s and 1940s did not give the ordinary man an unmediated voice. These are films that show the diversity of British regional accents in an unscripted way, allowing men to talk openly if under an obvious wartime censorship, for the first time. They also demonstrate a sense of place in the British Isles both in the origin of the men in the films and the cinemas in which they were shown, and covered all parts of the United Kingdom even though only a small part of those films survive. By a quirk of fate, the majority of reels that remain are from the Manchester area, but a wide variety of Lancashire accents are represented within them, from inner city Salford and Moss Side to the broader Lancastrian tones of Rochdale and Oldham and the more Liverpool inflected accents of Warrington and

St Helens. Other areas that have several films representing them include Dundee and Glasgow, Sheffield, the South Coast and Brighton, but in other films the dialects of Norfolk, Worcester, Birkenhead, Leicester and others are also preserved as they were spoken three generations ago. Sadly, there is a large part of the United Kingdom from which films have not apparently survived, including the whole of London, Northern Ireland and Wales.

But the films reveal much that is not overt in the standard form of wartime message the men delivered. The men were not censored, however much they would have been aware of what could not be spoken, and many use the opportunity to express their true feelings or create a kind of scripted performance that subtly and ironically undermines the official form. Men speak openly from the heart to their wives: 'Be in God's keeping' (*CB* 52 1944), 'My love for you will never die' (*CB* 86 1944) or their hopes for a future after the war – 'Well son, this is the first time you've ever seen me, or heard me talk; I hope to be with you and take you fishing and all those things you want me to do' (*CB* 56 1944). More rarely they give a sardonic glimpse of their conditions – 'It's a real gradely place for anybody, to *die in*' (*CB* 210 1945). And in the background behind the men, or in noises off, a parallel and illuminating counter image reveals itself. In some films, the soundtrack is interrupted by machine gun fire or explosions, leaving the men seemingly unperturbed, and occasionally the devastation of combat is apparent through a background of bombed buildings in Mandalay or a destroyed bridge across the Irrawaddy River. However, despite the empire-based nature of the Allied Army – of the 690,000 men over 600,000 were from India and other countries of the British Empire (McLynn 2011: 1) – the Indians and other nationalities are rarely glimpsed in these films except literally in the background, as servants in the recreated NAAFI canteen or as civilians in the wartime locations. To look at the films through contemporary eyes, this erasure of the nations of the Empire fighting troops, the East and West Africans, the Gurkhas, Karen, West Indians and the Burmese themselves, seems jarring. Only traces and hints for the most part of wartime attitudes to the multinational force and its multi-ethnic composition remain to be decoded in the present.

The films were made with the highest production values and most advanced technologies of the day – 35mm camera film and high-quality synchronized sound. The location Akeley camera, a famous piece of apparatus used by leading documentarists like Robert Flaherty, when fitted with the sound on film module, was the most advanced 'portable' sync sound camera of its time. The results when seen on screen eight decades later are still astonishing – crisp, well-lit cinema quality images and hi fidelity recorded voices. It is partly this that reinforces their significance today, a sense of time compressed, of the ordinary man in the heightened theatre of wartime, elevated through these high definition moving images and sounds. They are not documentaries but have

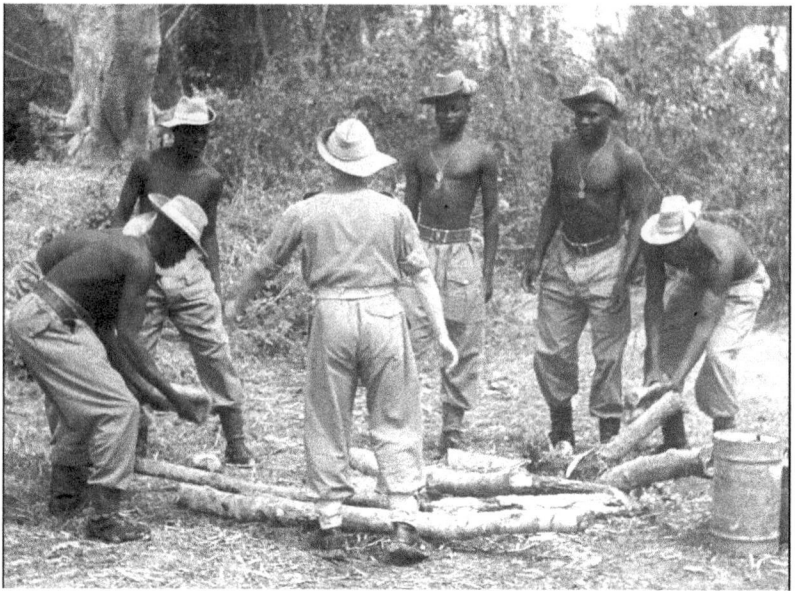

FIGURE I.2: The East African Division after serving in the Kadaw Valley ('Death Valley') (*CB* 199 1945). © IWM.

some of the features of wartime documentary, given, however, the production values of feature film. But their significance also lies in what is not said, and what seeps unintended into the portrayal of men who had to downplay the conditions under which they were filmed – 'It's a bit warm' (*CB 203 1945*). 'We're still knocking Johnny Jap for six' (*CB 212 1945*).

It is a curious fact that this denial of their wartime experience lasted almost invariably into peacetime and, as their families bore witness, across the whole of their lives. Again and again close relatives tell of men who never spoke of their war, even when their role in the conflict had been significant or heroic. Silences, as Jay Winter has pointed out, can be meaningful and revealing in their own right (Winter 2017: 176). Sometimes events were too terrible to recall, sometimes they are a fitting memorial to the departed, such as the one minute's silence at the football ground, and often they are necessary just to enable the daily compromises and practicalities of family life to carry on. These silences seem characteristic of a particular generation, but have been gradually unpicked by more recent generations who are determined to make sense of family networks, in the context of what has been called the 'memory boom' (Winter 2006: 1) of the last few decades, and the popularity of media productions such as *Who Do You Think You Are?*. Many families have a deep desire to retrace the past, to find faded ancestral footprints, evidence of lost relatives, in order to make sense of the present, and the films are the first in history where large numbers of living and speaking grandfathers and great grandfathers can be encountered directly and powerfully. It was partly to connect with this deep desire, that the author originated with the director of the North West Film Archive, Marion Hewitt, recreations of the wartime screenings, where we traced the living relatives of the men on screen and then invited them to contemporary screenings of the films, in regional cinemas just as they would have been done in wartime, in Manchester, Sheffield, Birkenhead and Brighton.

We know from contemporary newspaper reports and the testimony of families who were there, that the original cinema screenings were highly emotional affairs, where laughter and tears mingled equally, as relatives saw for the first time, often after many years apart, their loved ones projected onto a large screen in their local picture house, such as the vast Regent cinema in the centre of Sheffield. In an era before camera phones, to appear on film in the cinema was unimaginable, and many of the men reference this – 'Yes it's really me, not Alfred Hitchcock or Mickey Mouse' (*CB* 85 1944). And this was the golden era of popular cinema-going, pre-television, where by 1945 thirty million people cinema tickets were sold every week (Farmer 2016: 11). There was a confusion, a blurring of the experience of escapist entertainment and the shock of seeing a father or husband in the same cinema on the large screen, where the very fact of being there in front of the image counteracted the effect of the, often stilted, delivery or the familiar nature of the message delivered.

The recreated screenings also took place in an atmosphere of heightened emotion, but this time augmented by a sense of remembrance, emphasized both in that nearly all the men had passed away in the intervening seven decades but also in the remembrance of World War II itself and in particular the Fourteenth Army. I make a case that the screenings can be seen as a kind of secular service, where personal family history and national history intermingle, and also that these events saw a remarkable and moving outpouring of stories about the men on screen from the relatives of the *Calling Blighty* men, some of whom were there as children in the audience the last time the films were screened during wartime. The men themselves were mostly reticent at the time about the momentous events they were living through, and this became a deliberate forgetting after the war, but more recently their relatives have a more compelling need to uncover the personal histories of their forebears.

This book represents a multidisciplinary study of the significance of these unique films, the first ever of their type. I view them through a number of lenses to reveal both the context in which they were made, how they came about and their meaning as seen from a number of viewpoints. There has been no monograph on the *Calling Blighty* films although there is an excellent article by Paul Sargent in the *Imperial War Museum Review* nearly 30 years ago, and this book builds on his research and insights. Apart from that the films usually merit a line or two in film histories of WWII, a footnote to wartime output that I argue belies their importance that outweighs the content of the messages themselves.

Chapter 1 looks at the background of the war in India and Burma between 1941 and 1946. It is impossible to completely comprehend why the films were produced, and the disjunction between the matter of fact manner of the men on screen and the conditions they faced in combat, without an understanding of the conflict in the Far East. And this phase of the war, if not an actual secret, is still little known in relation to the other theatres of war in World War II. Few feature films deal with it, popular TV surveys of the war tend to miss it out and the reasons for the British involvement in Burma are only dimly if at all known about by a general audience. This is in contrast to the US involvement in the Pacific war, still now being represented, not to say glamourized by feature films and popular media histories.

The late British Burma veteran and fundraiser Captain Sir Tom Moore rightly captured the public imagination with his walks for charity and his war service in Burma, but very few of the media portrayals in print or TV focused on the reality of his war, or its colonial echoes (he was training Indian Army motorcyclists). I explore this hidden conflict through acknowledged sources but also the voices and the writing of the men who actually appear in the *Calling Blighty* films, especially Tag Barnes, a Sheffield man who wrote an insightful memoir of his own commando war.

The history of Burma is also little known despite its regular reappearance in the news, and unlike many ex-colonies, there are no echoes of its food and culture in the British high street. At the time of writing, Myanmar (Burma) has been rocked by yet another military coup, and the war and its aftermath have left a long and hopeless legacy on the country. Chapter 1 also considers the litany of failure in the war against the Japanese, the prevalence of disease and the extraordinarily hard conditions on everyday life and combat and the often dysfunctional military organisation. It considers the differing aims of the United States and British within the Fourteenth army, both as an attempt to reclaim a lost colony and also a bulwark to support Chinese allies.

Chapter 2 examines the ecology of wartime film and how the *Calling Blighty* films fit into the output of documentary and fiction, at this apogee of popular cinemagoing. It looks at how the films shared some of the qualities of the newsreel and documentary but also stood apart from them and the place of cinema in this pre-television age. In particular, the chapter considers the meagre output of fiction and non-fiction films about Burma both during and after the war and the reasons for this: the conflict between US and British aims, the failure in the war up to 1944 and the lack of a straightforward heroic narrative. The iconic documentaries of the 1930s and 1940s are well covered, in such texts as Elizabeth Sussex's *The Rise and fall of British Documentary* (1975) and class and language in film in Jo Fox's *Millions Like Us* (2006). Cinemagoing itself, then at its height, is fully dealt with in Richard Farmer's *Cinemas and Cinemagoing in Wartime Britain* (2016), and the general context in Aldgate and Richards's *Britain can Take it* (1994) and S.P. Mackenzie's *British War Films 1939–45* (2001). But none of these sources mention the *Calling Blighty* films at all, despite their running time, the equivalent of 40 full length feature films, and that they were screened in cinemas. It may be that they are just little known about or considered as living letters rather than films, something this book aims to address.

Chapter 3 examines how the films came about, a contested field, as there have been differing claims in the past as to who was responsible for the initial idea. But I also look at the reasons for the existence of the films in the first place, in the Far East war; how a sense of invisibility coupled with technological advances in film led to their creation. How the immense distances involved from the United Kingdom heightened a sense of being left behind, plus a lack of other amenities such as NAAFI clubs, radios, beer, but crucially also regular and swift mail communication. And I reveal how a former BBC children's presenter came up with the idea and harnessed the extensive resources necessary to enable films of almost 8000 men, around a tenth of the whole UK force, to be shot in the most difficult conditions and screened back in Blighty.

Chapter 4 is an overview of the messages, which despite their standard pattern and the unspoken limits of censorship manage to convey much about men in wartime. The differences between the (constructed studio) NAAFI film location and the films made in the war zone in Burma and how contemporary advanced film camera and sound on film recording technologies made them possible. The intimacy of the second-person address direct to camera, completely normalized to a present-day audience through smartphones, but then highly unusual, especially in the cinema. And how the largely unknown directors created filmic situations and shaped rudimentary narratives from the unpromising basic setups to camera. I focus also on the regionality of the films, in the accents and local references of the men (unknown at the time when documentary film was dominated by upper-middle class filmmakers) and their significance as the first exposure in cinema of the informal working-class voice.

In Chapter 5 I examine how masculinity is portrayed in the films, and how this fits within a body of self-authored narratives by men in war; the soldier's tale. In particular, how the stiff upper lip role model of men in WWII, plus the need to reassure those at home, and their own self-censorship shaped their self-portrayal on screen. How the messages have antecedents: written messages from men in war almost from the dawn of war itself. Many generations of soldiers' letters exist from the time onward of greater literacy in the late Victorian period, and examples can still be read that go back even further. But a letter or a photograph is a different experience to a moving image. The messages home could elide the truth as Tag Barnes shows but could also reveal past the formalities of conventional self-representation, elements of sexuality and ironic humour. I look at the few messages from women, much less represented within the *Calling Blighty* output but surprisingly similar to the male conventions. Overall what comes through from memories of the men as recounted by their relatives is silence, or a body of silences, about their experiences and the need to forget, and I examine the reasons for this.

Chapter 6 deals with the legacy and portrayal of the colonial troops who made up the vast majority of the 14th Army. Invisible for the most part they were relegated literally to the background of filmed scenes where a British soldier was in the foreground, either as servants, cameramen or exotic local colour. I look at the role of the Commonwealth troops, how this role has only recently become publicly recognized, and especially the Indian, Gurkha and even African troops, the latter sent many thousands of miles from their homeland to fight for the seat of Empire and defend a distant colony. How East African troops were unfairly portrayed in surviving *Calling Blighty* films, and how racism pursued US troops from their own homeland. This chapter builds on Yasmin Khan's comprehensive background to the field in books such as *The Raj at war* (2015). Some British men in the films do show responsiveness to the surrounding culture, partly evidenced by the Hindi slang spoken on screen, but others felt a profound sense of alienation. Nor was the position of the Indian and Burmese population completely uniform, as shown by support for the anti-British Indian and Burmese national armies.

Chapter 7 considers the films within a pattern of remembrance of men and war in the twentieth century and afterwards. Building on Jay Winter's writings and especially *War beyond Words* (2017), I classify three ways of representing film as memorial. Firstly the popular media memorial usually demonstrated by broadcast television but also in feature film, then ritual ceremony as exemplified by Remembrance Day but also within the recreated film screenings of the *Calling Blighty* films and their characterization as a kind of secular service, and finally critical reflection, where a more nuanced critical gaze is focused on memory, especially through the creative reuse of archive film. I look at how we memorialize the dead in the public imagination through events as well as cemetery headstones, with a mixture of truth and comforting illusion. The heroic warrior myth is not contradicted by the recreated screenings, which are surprisingly similar to the original showings to relatives in the mid-1940s in their format and reactions, and mixture of laughter and tears. I also look at the response to the *Calling Blighty* films identified as part of the 'memory boom' of the late twentieth century, mixed with a strong desire to connect with past relatives. The conclusion then draws these threads together and tries to place these unique films in their historical context and to judge just how their significance can be assessed.

For the general contemporary audience, the films are a fascinating confrontation with the past, but for relatives they have a more complex meaning. The ritual of making visible fathers and their varied narratives can often have a healing dimension, making sense of a past previously denied. Just as there were some things that the men could say but others that must be left unsaid, so in acts of remembrance there are things that can and cannot be uttered. The films once discovered (they were not hidden but often overlooked in scattered regional and national archives) had wide national appeal and were featured in many radio and TV broadcasts. Channel 4 television in the UK broadcast an hour-long documentary *Messages Home, Lost Films of the British Army* (2016), about the men and the films, and our recreated screenings, and I consider how these can be regarded, truthful but constrained by our attitudes towards remembrance. Above all, the films are considered as the remarkable and unique documents they are, a powerful mix of art, memorials to those lost over the decades and a regional film census of men from across the United Kingdom, caught on film for the first time. Memories of love in a time of war that gain power and significance as the years roll by.

1

Death and Disease in the Jungle: The War in Burma

I understand you believe you're the forgotten army. That's not true.
The truth is nobody's ever bloody well heard of you!

(Lord Louis Mountbatten, Far East Commander, addressing
men in Burma in 1943 [WW2today 2016: n.pag.])

Fought from December 1941 to August 1945, the war in Burma against the Japanese was the longest continuous campaign fought by the British, along with their much more numerous allies, colonial troops from India, Africa, as well as the United States and China and many local tribes. From many viewpoints, it was

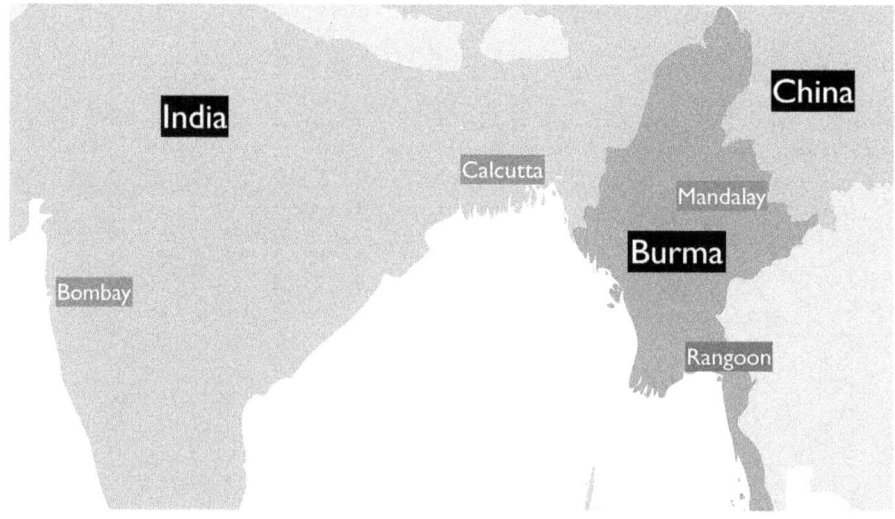

FIGURE 1.1: Burma and India in 1940. © Steve Hawley.

also the most terrible, a 'great, if puzzling and tragic enterprise' (Allan 1984: xx), marked by a cruel and at first seemingly invincible enemy, the will-sapping and alien conditions of heat and the boot rotting monsoon and the inevitability of tropical disease, which at one point caused 200 cases of sickness for every battle casualty (Rothwell 2016: 1).

In addition, it was founded on humiliating failure, with the fall of the British colony of Singapore and the capture of 60,000 Commonwealth troops (some estimate many more); Churchill called it the largest capitulation in British military history. For the following two years, there was precious little cheer for a home population, with defeat or stalemate at best against the Japanese in jungle warfare, despite the propaganda value of smaller-scale guerrilla expeditions by Brigadier Orde Wingate's Chindits, which themselves incurred heavy losses.

It was against this background of distance, disease and defeat that the *Calling Blighty* films came into being, a way of addressing the slow transmission of the servicemen's written messages home and making physical the images and speech of the men serving far away. They arose from a sense of invisibility, a lack of morale among the British troops, men who perceived themselves as overlooked even on active service in wartime. The description of the Forgotten Army was taken to heart by the South East Asia Command, and they, partly bitterly, and partly with pride, have referred to themselves by the epithet up to the present day. In order to boost morale and create a sense of visibility to contradict that, the unprecedented project was conceived, the first time it had ever been attempted, and at a huge scale, in a theatre of war 5000 miles from home and using for that time innovative technology. Just to gather the men from different cities and countries together was logistically problematic in wartime with a lack of air transport, and it is extraordinary that by the end of filming around 8000 men and women had delivered their messages in cinemas all around the United Kingdom.

Despite the disease, the risk of death, and the raw horror of the conflict, almost none of the men in the film referred to the terrible nature of the war they were engaged in: the films were intended after all to reassure their relatives at home, to smooth over the unthinkable and provide hope and project normality. The reality of their war and how it fitted into the Burma campaign as a whole is almost entirely absent, and nor was it hardly ever revealed post-war, where, as we will see, the dominant mode of response was one of silence. However, there is one example where we can trace with some accuracy the hidden active service of one of the soldiers in the films.

Ernest 'Tag' Barnes was a landscape gardener in Sheffield for much of his life before going into the fishing tackle industry, to chime with his lifelong hobby of fishing and hunting. In 1942, he was serving in the Yorks and Lancs Regiment and later the Royal Artillery and had what he called a cushy job, devising training programmes for new recruits. Restless, he volunteered for the Commandos and embarked on 'a second lifetime encapsulated into three and a half years' (Barnes 1991: 13). He is unique amongst the men appearing in the surviving *Calling Blighty* films, in that he both kept diaries throughout the war ('I don't think you were supposed to, but I did') and then, 45 years after the war ended, used them as a basis for his war memoir, *Commando Diary* (1991). He is therefore one of the few who break the silence, and we can also compare the contemporary events and thoughts of his war service with his rather laconic appearance in the film – he even mentions the occasion in his book: 'A little more than a month after leaving Bombay I was back there again with a couple of comrades to take part in a greeting film which was to be sent back to Britain' (Barnes 1991: 67). Tag's film, like many and perhaps the majority of films, was shot in what appeared to be a NAAFI canteen, which was in fact a constructed set in the Shree Sound Studios in Bombay, where men from Sheffield had been flown to and grouped together to deliver their messages before they returned to their bases at the front.

His message to his family in Sheffield is fairly typical of the general pattern; he is called away from a darts match (a common trope in the Bombay studio films) and with a cigarette in hand greets his parents and girlfriend. 'Hope you're all okay. I'm getting your mail regularly now so I'm okay [...] and congratulations to Dad on winning the fishing club prize, good show that. So keep smiling, and keep your pins in'. He also apologises to his then girlfriend 'I'm sorry I can't be

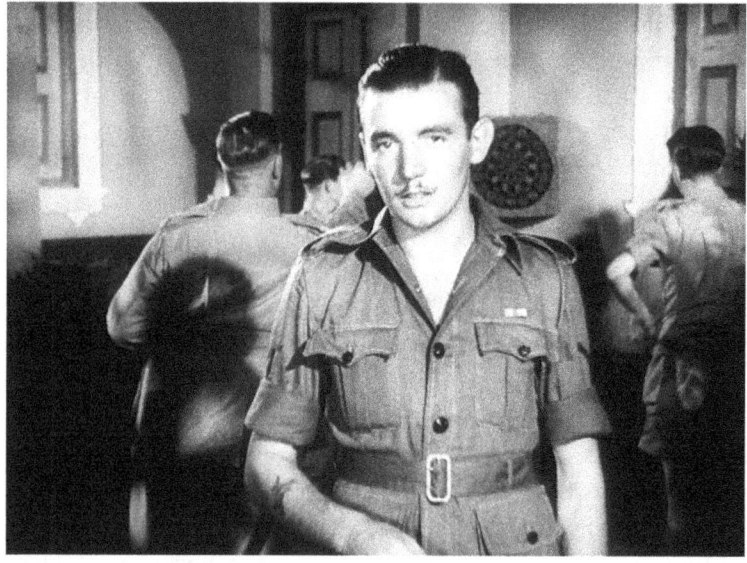

FIGURE 1.2: 'Tag' Barnes. 'Congratulations to Dad on winning the fishing club prize' (*CB* 86 1944). © BFI.

home for our anniversary this year but maybe I'll manage it next year and we'll toddle off to Blackpool' (*CB* 86 1944). There is little indication of the action he had already engaged in as a commando in North Africa or Italy but also no hint he was also to play a key role in the famous battle at Hill 170 on the Arakan peninsular in Burma, where he won the Military Medal. The life of the soldier is vividly depicted in the memoir, the fierce loyalty to comrades, the monotony and chaotic organization, the heat and disease, interspersed with brief but intense periods of action. He also and more unusually describes his frequent sexual adventures and opportunities for fishing (he eventually became a well-known writer on angling) and birdwatching: 'In retrospect the [wintering hen harriers] may have been the much rarer Montague's harrier' (Barnes 1991: 33).

Barnes's memoir provides a fascinating commentary on the ordinary soldier during the Burma campaign. In fact with his battle honours, his own war was perhaps rather more extraordinary, and he did not arrive in Bombay until January 1944, by which time the campaign had already lasted two years. His message and the way it is delivered are completely unremarkable, and there is a total disconnection between the turbulent events he was living through and participating in and the calm poise of his words. Since the fall of Singapore in February 1942 when he was in his 'cushy' army job in Britain, the war had been waged fruitlessly in the jungles of Burma. The causes of the campaign he fought in were complex and perhaps not fully understandable at the time, but at their core, they were essentially economic rather than political.

The British had acquired the country of Burma almost piecemeal over a century, and despite its economic usefulness to the Empire, it had always been considered a province of India, with little or no consideration of its own ethnic or political sensitivities. The first British incursion had ended badly, with the massacre at Negrais in the mid-1750s, when the first trading station failed from disease and attacks from the Burmese. A series of wars from the 1820s onwards led to the occupation of the country in stages; in the first assault by the East India Company forces Rangoon was taken, after victory against the war elephants and muskets of the King of Ava. Following the third and final war against King Thikaw of upper Burma in 1885, the country was incorporated into the British Empire, but it was always something of an imperial backwater, ruled from India, although with limited self-government from 1932 onwards. As an Indian province, akin to the Punjab or Bengal, it had little cultural importance of its own to the Empire, although its value in terms of trade and natural resources had grown substantially over the decades of colonialization.

Burma was rich in rice (the Irrawaddy delta became the greatest rice producer in the world), timber, oil and minerals: the wulfram mine in Mauchi produced one-third of the world's wulfram, also known as the ultra-hard element tungsten.

There were also oil wells, timber, mining and rubber resources. British and especially Glasgow merchants dominated trade in the colony, leaving to this day in the country a legacy of golf courses, the taste for scotch whisky and even the playing of the bagpipes by Kachin rebels in the north (Myint-U 2008: n.pag.). But whilst the British had built roads, hospitals and irrigation schemes (McLynn 2011: 7), they had little interest in the language, customs or folklore in this appendix to India and endured the conditions of heat, disease and the monsoon for the possibilities of exploiting the country's natural resources.

As landowners and the merchant class from India and China immigrated to Burma, the traditional society, already splintered through ethnic divisions of the Burmans, Karens, Shans and hill tribes, began to disintegrate. Independence became an aim for the disenfranchised Burmese, and many cheered when the Japanese invaded in 1941, some even joining the pro-independence and pro-Japanese army of General Aung San (the father of Nobel Prize winner and State Counsellor or Prime Minister of present-day Myanmar, Aung San Suu Kyi). To this day, there are few cultural echoes in Britain of Burma's century or more within the Empire. Burma is not part of the Commonwealth, there are no Burmese restaurants in British high streets, few British have ever visited the country, and there is little curiosity about the shared cultural history, unlike that of India or Australia or the African former colonies. If Burma is known about at all in the United Kingdom, it may be because George Orwell was stationed there as a military policeman or the distant memories of the Forgotten Army in WWII. Orwell spent five years in the country in the 1920s as a policeman in the Indian imperial police stationed in the Irrawaddy Delta. He wrote the novel *Burmese Days* (1934) about his experiences, and although he liked the country itself and the beauty of its landscape, he hated the imperialism he found there and felt only disgust for his part in the British Colonial System. In an essay he wrote later under his real name, Eric Blair, 'How a nation is exploited', he 'showed the methods the British Empire uses to milk dry Asian colonies'. He describes the countryside as an earthly paradise but savagely criticizes Britain's imperial despotism disguised as democracy and predicts in essence the move towards independence that would come two decades later (Blair 1929: n.pag.).

The Japanese too were interested in Burma – as an economic resource, its oil, rice and rubber were important, but it was not their primary goal, it was also a stepping stone to India and a buffer to the Chinese in the north. The war in Burma was part of a wider conflict that raged over Asia, which predominantly pitted the Japanese Empire against the United States but also Great Britain and the other western allies. Japan had invaded Manchuria in 1931 and continued in 1937 with an attack on China. Tension had been building in any case between the Japanese and the United States, where the Japanese Empire felt that through the Monroe doctrine, South and North America were barred to them economically, but no such scruples were felt by the Americans in terms of their own economic expansion into the Far East. President Franklin Delano Roosevelt was (some felt myopically) wedded to China and especially the corrupt nationalist leader Chang Kai-shek, a futile and uncritical blind spot that continued throughout World War II and led to billions of dollars worth of resources pouring into Chang's regime in Chungking through Burma over the mountains, the famous 'hump'.

The hawks in the Japanese military and navy had increasing sway over national policy, but Burma was never the primary target for expansion, rather the oil of the Dutch East Indies – present-day Indonesia – and the rubber and tin of the British colony of Malaya (Allen 1984: 5). In order to displace the China-focused United States as the dominant Pacific power and enlarge its natural resources in Southeast Asia, the infamous attack on the US Pacific Fleet at Pearl Harbor, Hawaii, was launched on 7 December 1941. Although 18 warships were sunk or damaged, crucially all three of the Pacific fleet's aircraft carriers were not at Pearl Harbour during the attack, and many of the other ships were repaired and re-entered service. Admiral Hara Tadaichi summed up the Japanese result by saying, 'We won a great tactical victory at Pearl Harbor and thereby lost the war' (Haufer 2003: 127). The hammer blow of the surprise attack had been deflected in its aim to destroy the fleet, but on the day after the attack, FDR declared war on Japan.

Burma was still not a primary objective, but the Japanese feared resistance from the British Army in India and hoped that insurrection in India would depose the British Raj, once their troops had reached Assam. In addition, they wanted to cut the overland route to China from Burma that supplied Chang Kai-shek's nationalist army in Chungking, along the famed Burma road. If this supply route could be closed, the Chinese nationalists would wither and allow Japanese expansion northwards to conquer the whole of China. In this, they further invited US intervention into Burma to join the British and Empire troops together with the more limited Chinese forces.

The ostensible unity of the 14th Army in Southeast Asia thus concealed two vastly different motives for the major Western protagonists in the Burma conflict. The British war in Burma was essentially a war to reclaim a lost colony, an attempt to retain the country for the Empire, fought by a Commonwealth army in which British troops were very much in the minority. The United States Burma war was, however, a quite different one, to liberate the Burma Road and supply Chang Kai-shek with materiel, in order to keep China in the war and strike Japan from there, but also to feed FDR's vision and emotional attachment to China in the post-war world. The Burma Road was eventually reopened and extended, at a tremendous cost of American, Indian and Burmese manpower, but it was almost too late. The war would soon be over, and aircraft had taken over from lorries and

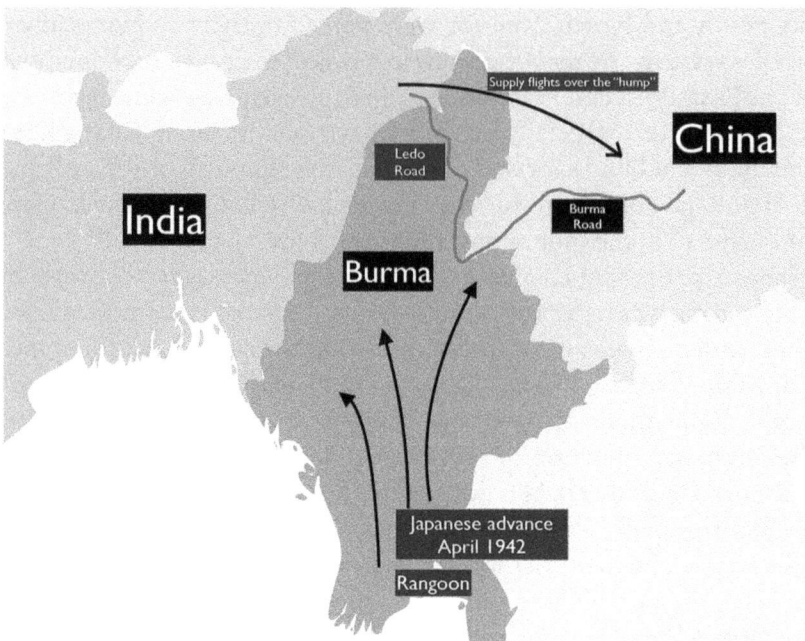

FIGURE 1.3: Map showing the Japanese invasion and the supply lines in Northern Burma. © Steve Hawley.

land vehicles, with endless flights over the 'hump' supplying more material, and much more quickly than could ever be taken by road. However, the war against the Japanese was to proceed slowly with setbacks and failure at the outset and defeat and stalemate persisted even into 1944; it was part of this inability of the British forces to make headway against an enemy who was eventually seen to the great surprise of the British as ruthless and surprisingly invincible, which led to the start of production of the *Calling Blighty* films in late 1943.

Entering Burma from Thailand after the fall of Singapore in January 1942, the Japanese rapidly overran Rangoon and cut off the Burma Road immediately at its origin. The supreme commander of the Far East theatre was General Sir Archibald Wavell, who in ordering his fighting formations well forward, left them dangerously exposed. In addition, the 17th division of 7000 men under Major-General Sir John Smyth, who commanded the Rangoon garrison, was either only trained for desert warfare or not trained or equipped at all (Allen 1984: 24). A defeat at Moulmein alarmed the British and was followed by further defeats and retreat. The Japanese were seasoned fighters, who infiltrated the jungle in small groups, travelling light on bicycles and equipped with small arms, whilst the British were handicapped by large trucks and full kit that rendered them slow to respond.

The Burcorps (Burma Corps) was created on 13 March 1942 to take control of the scattered British and Indian troops retreating in a haphazard way from the Japanese back to India, and command was taken over by the dynamic Lieutenant-General William Slim. Slim was a career officer who had served in the Great War and had become a captain in the British Indian Army; despite spending most of the interwar years in administrative service roles, he gained the reputation in Burma of being a brilliant military strategist and extraordinary human being. The Burma Corps opened up a scorched earth policy as it fell back up the Irrawaddy River, accompanied by tens of thousands of Indian refugees, themselves harassed severely by the local Burmese population. A last-ditch attempt to take Rangoon by the British had almost resulted in disaster, but the counterattacking Japanese unblocked the road north and allowed the troops to retreat, but not before the British had destroyed nearly 1000 US lend-lease trucks and £11 million worth of the Burmah oil company's installations in the city (McLynn 2011: 27). In May 1942, the retreat finally ended, and nearly all the troops of Burcorps had crossed into India after a nearly 1000-mile trek, but the cost had been immense. In addition to 13,000 dead and wounded British servicemen, an estimated 100,000 Indians of the million who had been resident in the country and were fleeing had died on the trek north; it was an ignominious situation, and after Singapore and the rout in Burma, there was little encouragement for a British public hungry for some success in the dark days of the war. What followed were many months of stalemate and the prospect of a bitter conflict to retake Burma, a country where there was only patchy support for the British to start with, and perhaps 5–10 per cent of Burmese were strongly pro-Japanese.

Tag Barnes paints a vivid and earthily realistic picture of the British Army and its operations in Burma from the point he landed there on 20 January 1944. He notes the mixture of dysfunctional Indian organization mirrored by that of the British Army: 'The chaotic state of the Indian railway system was totally unbelievable. If one was fortunate the waiting time might be less than two hours' (Barnes 1991: 52). Already in the first few days, the men were being struck down by illness, some with malaria and others with dysentery; the troops made tea from water in a well and then found that Indian boys with sores as big as half crowns on their legs had been swimming in it. The prevalence of disease both in India and Burma was a serious problem for the 14th Army, and incapacity due to illness was many times more common than that due to battle injury. By 1943, malaria had an incidence rate of 84% in the Indian army (Allen 1984: 182), but a raft of other unpleasant diseases was common and they were all debilitating. Typhoid, cholera, blackwater fever, the dysentery mentioned by Tag Barnes, plus numerous skin diseases and a special kind of jungle typhus spread by mites, wreaked havoc with the Indian soldiers and the British alike. Ben Macrae of the Norfolk Regiment noted later 'You got dysentery from the water, it had to be chlorinated, but there was a permanent state of dysentery. It was a waste of time going sick. To get sunburnt was a criminal army offence so you were told to protect yourself' (McRae 1997: n.pag.). And Dick Fiddament from Norfolk also observed 'The Indians and the Burmese, part of the British Empire, they didn't want us. On top of this you had malaria, dengue fever, prickly heat, jungle sores, dysentery; this is why you got despondent' (Fiddament 1997: n.pag.).

General Slim was a believer in modern medicine and took measures to halt the spread of illness, which was severely impacting on the army's fighting ability. Mosquito nets and insect repellents were issued to the troops (Allen 1984: 104), but the greatest impact came through a new 'wonder' drug, mepacrine, which was issued to all troops and gradually reduced the incidence of malaria. It was not popular with the men despite its usefulness; it turned the skin yellow and was widely rumoured to be a kind of bromide to reduce sexual activity. Nonetheless, this and a variety of measures, including treating illness at the front instead of evacuating invalided soldiers back behind the front line to the safety of India, had a gradual but powerful effect on the scourge of tropical disease. By 1944, the sickness rate had been reduced to 20 to 1 for each battle casualty and by 1945 to 6 to 1 (Rothwell 2016: 1). But this still meant a high proportion of men were ill at any one time, and the chance of serving in the Far East without succumbing was virtually negligible. Slim himself caught malaria in 1945; disobeying his own rules, he took a bath after sunset and was bitten by mosquitoes (Slim 1956: 104).

It was not long before Ernest Barnes, still far from Burma, came down with dysentery; during a raft-building exercise, he passed out and was taken to Poona hospital with a temperature of 105°F and a dangerously high pulse rate. Indian orderlies fanned him with wet blankets, and he gradually recovered after eight days, just in time to experience the other characteristic of tropical warfare, the fierce and overpowering monsoon rainstorms. Military operations for both sides were dramatically affected by the tropical monsoon, which falls from mid-March to mid-October. Tag's first encounter with it came in March 1944 as 'torrential rain fell, accompanied by the fiercest wind experienced; tents were whipped away like pieces of rag, and extra-large tent pegs, considered to hold out against anything, were wrenched out as if they were matchsticks. It was a further three days before any training could be considered' (Barnes 1991: 54).

The terrible nature of disease combined with the monsoon was bad enough during training, but as Slim describes, during operations on the grim retreat to India after the Japanese took Rangoon, it took on the nature of a plague of biblical proportions. 'Ploughing their way up over slopes, over a track inches deep in slippery mud, soaked to the skin, rotten with fever, ill-fed and shivering [...] their only rest at night was to lie on sodden ground under the dripping trees, without even a blanket to cover them' (Slim 1956: 109).

Tag was to suffer recurring bouts of dysentery, returning to the hospital in India, plus hornet stings requiring a morphine injection, and this was all in the first few weeks in India before operations had begun. However, as a determined naturalist, he was still able to get in some fishing, 'and on one occasion hooked a fish which put up a tremendous fight – like a bull on a pole. It was a barbel-like looking specimen of about five pounds, which someone said was mahseer'. Thoughts of home recurred but not without irony; after a seven-mile hike in the relentless heat (one daytime temperature reached 136°F), and as they prepared for an all-night exercise, 'recollection was made that at the time the miners in Britain were on strike complaining about low wages!' (Barnes 1991: 56). Other soldiers remembered later the physical conditions of warfare in Burma. Ben Macrae reflected on the monsoon: 'the night it did come down it laid flat everything in the camp. It just came down in solid sheets of water. Down they came [the tents]' (McRae 1997: n.pag.). The relentless heat took its toll, and the coolest place was the officers' mess, which was over 127 degrees in the shade in the afternoon. McRae estimated that outside under the tarpaulins where they serviced vehicles must have been 140 degrees. Dick Fiddament, who appeared in a *Calling Blighty* film, 'had a bad time with roundworm. In the monsoon season, incessant rain, until you've actually been there, there's no comparison. You're out there in a little hole in the ground, and protected with the monsoon cape, which was virtually useless. You begin to get the ague, shaky and cold. You're thoroughly dejected and you think to yourself if there's one with my name on it bloody good job' (Fiddament 1997: n.pag.).

In Tag Barnes's camp in Cocanda in the Bay of Bengal, the situation looked idyllic, but disease was rife with large queues outside the medical centre, mostly for malaria and dysentery but also numerous skin complaints; ringworm and dhobi itch, plus the threat of elephantiasis in the nearby village. But the birdlife was rich and varied, as he notes, and not only were there vultures and hawks but also 'rather beautiful Brahminy kites' (Barnes 1991: 59). Morale, which was a prime motivator in the creation of the *Calling Blighty* films, was fragile. After the opening of the second front in Europe on June 6th, there was a strong and almost indescribable feeling of having being left behind. The men's private thoughts were of home and family but tempered in Tag's case by frustration as to whether they should ever meet the Japanese in action. In the meantime, there were other diversions, discussed frankly in Barnes's memoir, but hardly unusual for men in wartime in the brothels of Grant Road, Bombay (which he never indulged in himself), where attractive well-built Indian ladies sat in endless small cubicles that lined the long road, behind half-inch steel bars. In a resort called Breach Candy, he meets a masseuse called Rita, who for an extra 15 rupees supplies welcome extras, and far from home, he becomes close to her, even rushing around to see her straight after the filming of his *Calling Blighty* message at the Shree Sound Studios. 'Unfortunately she had left two days earlier to spend a holiday with her aunt in Bangalore!' (Barnes 1991: 67).

After the retreat from Rangoon to India, there had followed a period of stalemate for the 14th Army. An advance ordered by Wavell into the Arakan peninsular on the coast of Burma had ended in bloody defeat and morale had sunk further. To revitalize the war effort and rebuild morale, Slim introduced air support both as an offensive military force and crucially employed air transport on a vast scale to keep men in inhospitable terrain supplied with arms and food. This also enabled the troops to be rapidly transported from one military front to another. Visits by ENSA parties and British entertainers were encouraged despite the huge distances from the United Kingdom, and some top performers like George Formby and Vera Lynn and even Noel Coward made the long journey to improve the state of mind of the men far from home.

It was against this background that the first Chindit forces, combined Gurkha and British troops under Brigadier Orde Wingate, made a guerrilla expedition against the Japanese in Burma. This had some military success, even at the expense of heavy losses, but was able to show that the Japanese were not invincible in jungle warfare and that they could be defeated under the right circumstances. Wingate's legacy was mixed. His successes were achieved at a debilitating cost, but their propaganda value was immense, and as in 1943 the Allied High Command was reorganised and the charismatic and well-connected Lord Louis Mountbatten replaced General Sir Archibald Wavell, the tide gradually turned. Mountbatten was able to cajole much-needed supplies for the 14th Army and used his influence to gain much greater air support. Slim asserted control in the field and the Army units could sit tight in forward positions, reinforced by air supplies whilst they defended against the Japanese, who themselves were suffering supply difficulties.

The key and now legendary battle was that of Kohima/Imphal, when in the spring of 1944 Japan launched an invasion of India, by springing an attack on the garrison town of Imphal in Manipur, a border province, to prevent a British return to India. In order to isolate Imphal from its supply base at Dimapur, the small village of Kohima became the site of some of the most ferocious fighting of World War II. The famous battle over the District Commissioner's tennis court led to severe casualties on both sides, where Allied and Japanese soldiers exchanged grenades and small arms fire separated only by the width of the court. The wider battle pitched 80,000 Japanese troops against a much smaller cohort of defenders; the siege lasted 64 days, but the Japanese lost 30,000 troops killed and were also eventually defeated on the Kohima/Imphal Road, which was reopened (McLynn 2011: 323). The Japanese were forced to retreat, but only 20,000 crossed the River Chindwin unscathed. The course of

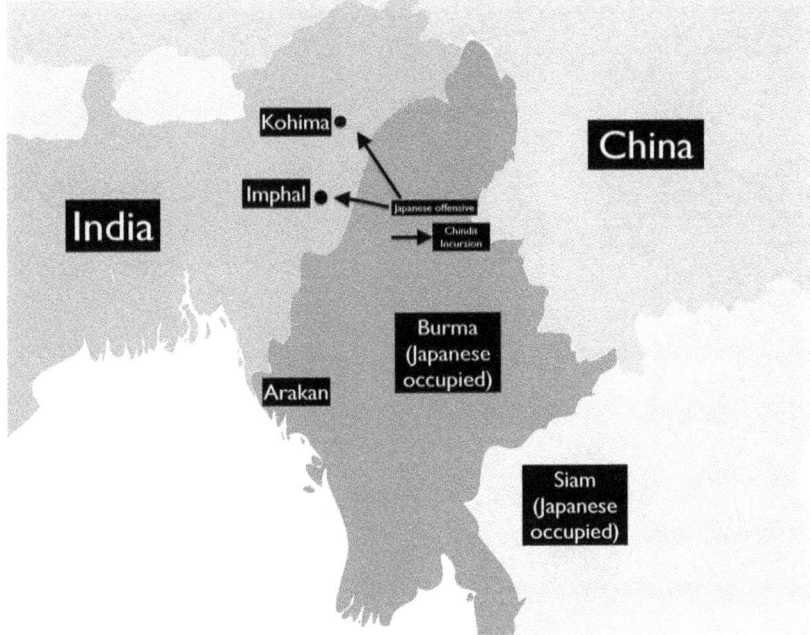

FIGURE 1.4: Burma 1944; the Japanese assault on Kohima/Imphal. © Steve Hawley.

the war had changed, also aided by a second allied offensive into the Arakan, in which Tag Barnes won his military medal, and a further Chindit incursion against the Japanese in the jungles of Burma.

Barnes was not the only man appearing in the *Calling Blighty* films who played a key military role in the tumultuous struggle to force the Japanese back out of Burma. Frank Miller was a private from Salford serving in the 2nd Battalion King's Own Royal Regiment from Lancashire, when he was filmed in 1945, probably in the grounds of the Shree studios in Bombay, sending a message to his wife. As part of the special forces, he had fought with Burmans and Gurkhas in the second Chindit incursion, 150 miles behind Japanese Lines, when 20,000 men under Wingate had attacked the enemy guerrilla fashion; many of the British troops were men from Lancashire. The story was told in the Channel 4 programme *Messages Home* (2016), when Miller's grandson spoke with military experts and a fellow Lancastrian who had also fought in the same battles. Casualties from the enemy and sickness were severe in the Chindit campaign and some questioned its effectiveness, but as contemporary newsreels related in the programme, the 'single most important achievement was to show that British troops can fight a jungle war better than the enemy'. Wingate tragically did not live to see the outcome as he was killed in a plane crash as the expedition began.

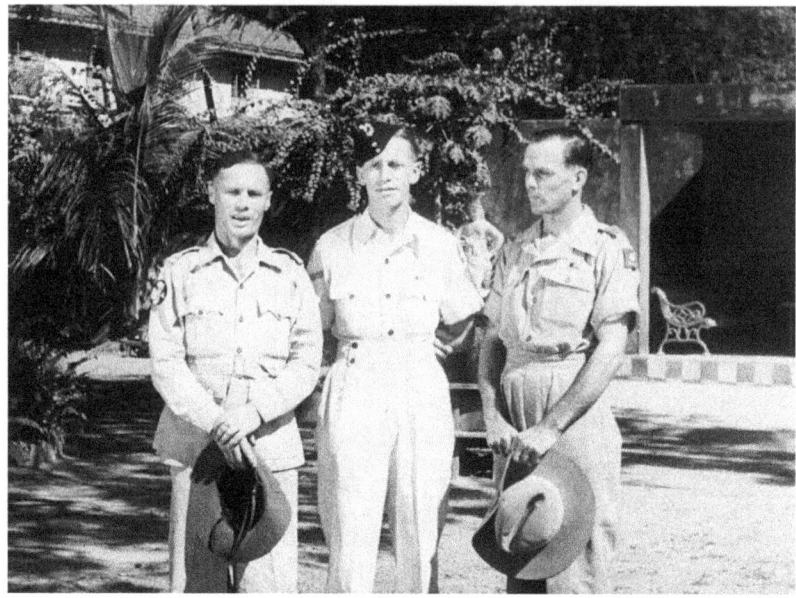

FIGURE 1.5: Frank Miller in Bombay wearing Chindit insignia (*CB* 273 1946). © IWM.

Between March and July 1944, the battles raged in Manipur and the Arakan in addition to Wingate's harassment behind the lines, but then the Japanese retreated in defeat across the Chindwin and the 14th Army advanced to chase them back through the open plains of Northern Burma. Mandalay fell in March, and the *Calling Blighty* cameras were there to film men of the Royal Norfolk and other regiments, seen in rare footage delivering their messages amid the ruins of the city, with their machine guns by their sides. The Japanese were harried out of the Arakan, and Rangoon was taken on the 3rd of May, which Mountbatten celebrated with an elaborate victory parade in June. But the fighting carried on, with many Japanese caught behind British lines, until the dropping of the US atomic bombs on Hiroshima and Nagasaki led to the Japanese surrender on the 15th of August 1945.

The conflict had been one of the most corrosive of the second war. Burma was one of the most difficult places on earth to fight a war, with its impenetrable jungle, steep and razor-sharp mountains, deep valleys and wide difficult rivers. The Japanese army, taken somewhat lightly by the British at the start of the invasion, soon became known as hardy and ruthless fighters. Capture and imprisonment by either side was not an option; as Ben Macrae recorded later for the Imperial War Museum 'You didn't take prisoners, God no, no. What, and feed them out of my rations? We knew that if you got taken prisoner you'd be used for bayonet practice. I never took any' (McRae 1997: n.pag.). Though Burma saw the bulk of the fighting, the effect on India was huge, as the country became a vast supply and training base during the war, as well as a springboard for many offensives against the Japanese.

The casualty rates in the Far East show startling discrepancies between the Japanese and British and Commonwealth forces. Whilst under 5000 troops of UK origin were killed in the conflict, and the total including Empire troops was nearly 15,000, the Japanese calculated that vastly more, over 185,000 of their men, had died in Burma (Allen 1984: 640). Many more Empire troops succumbed to tropical diseases, but the Burmese civilian population may have suffered the greatest toll, with perhaps one million lost to warfare, forced labour by the Japanese and the famine and disease that went along with the chaos of war (McLynn 2011: 1). For all those involved, it was a cruel and punishing war, little known about at the heart of the Empire in Britain, but remembered generations later through the survival of many of the *Calling Blighty* films and in the words of the British servicemen and a few women whose filmed messages bring to life the human face of the Forgotten Army. But although the war ended in August 1945, the weary task of clearing the country of remaining Japanese troops and of waiting for scarce transport back home, meant that repatriation for many men took months and even a year to fully implement. For this reason, the *Blighty* message films continued to be produced well into 1946, when in April of that year, the final issue number 391, of Brighton men, was filmed on Malabar Hill Bombay. One resigned Brighton soldier Peter Smith spoke for all his comrades when he said 'I like everyone else out here, am just waiting for the day to go home' (*CB* 391 1946). It would be many decades before the *Calling Blighty* films were again screened publicly, and the men from India and Burma were once more be seen in cinemas (and on television) back in Britain.

2

The Ecology of Wartime Film

There are scenes depicting the horrible atrocities the Japanese committed in one small village, but this is not merely a propaganda film; a stirring story, with its strange Oriental love, provides the theme. Relatives of Hull men in India heard and saw them on the screen in the supporting feature Calling Blighty.

(*Hull Daily Mail* 1945: 50, on *Dragon Seed*,
with Katherine Hepburn, and support)

It has become commonplace to consider World War II as the golden age of British cinema, and there is some truth in that. In terms of cinemagoing, there were a remarkable 31 million cinema visits a week by 1946 (Richards and Sheridan 1987: 12). But the war period was also the apogee of the British documentary movement, and the cinema newsreel was the chief audio-visual means whereby the average person received their (highly filtered) news. In addition, training and propaganda films were all intended to be seen in often makeshift cinemas and film shows, and taken together the role of film in the working, public and entertainment lives of the average citizen including servicemen and women, was immense. Rather presciently and unusually, in the surviving Birkenhead *Calling Blighty* film one man says 'Pity this is only one way, but maybe we will have television one of these days' (*CB* 266 1946). In fact, television broadcasts had begun in Britain in the late 1920s, but apart from a few experiments, they were only one way. The world's first high-definition TV Service had started in 1936, broadcast by the BBC, but it had been suspended in 1939 amid fears that the VHF transmissions would act as guidance beams for enemy bombers trying to locate central London (Timeline of the BBC 2020: n.pag.). The number of television sets at closedown was estimated at just 20,000 (9000 had been sold in London for the first TV outside broadcast (the coronation of King George VI) (A Short History of British television 2011: n.pag.). Practically speaking, this was a pre-television age, when the moving image was dominated in all its forms by film.

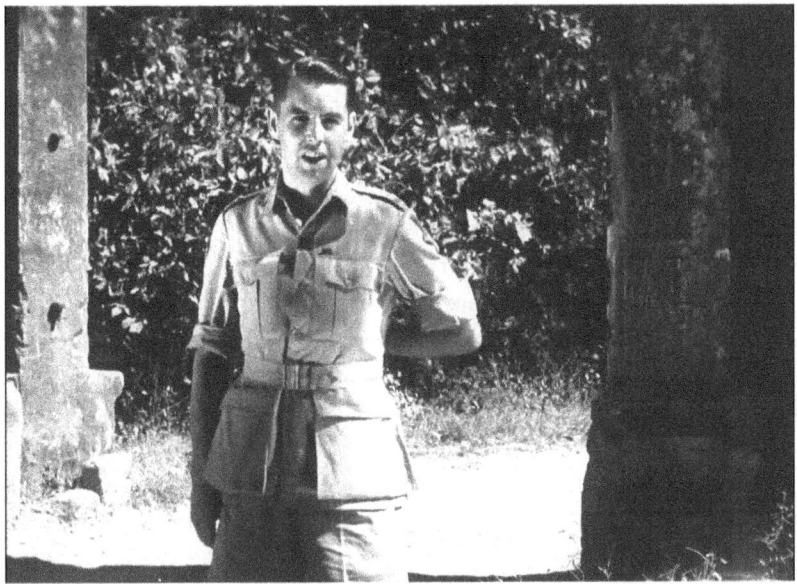

FIGURE 2.1: *Calling Blighty* Birkenhead 'Pity this is only one way, but maybe we'll all have television one of these days' (*CB* 266 1946). © IWM.

The *Calling Blighty* films were screened in public cinemas and often shown as a first short before the main feature; at least one of their makers considered them entertainments. They had grown out of the newsreel shorts in some ways and used similar recording equipment to the newsreels especially on location, and they also had something in common with pre-war and wartime documentary in their depiction of the ordinary man on screen. There were elements of all these in the films, but as one-way messages they were also unique, and their makers had to find their own language to convey the sense they were trying to portray. It is surprising in the age of Skype, where the close or medium close-up is the basic and intimate screen unit of communication, how few of the *Blighty* films are recorded in big close-up; presumably to convey the physical health of the man overseas and the implied comfort of their surroundings, a medium or wide shot was used mostly, thereby forgoing some intimacy.

The Army Kinematograph Service (AKS) was one component in a complex and intertwined web of non-fiction wartime filmmaking, which also included the Ministry of Information (Films division) that had been formed in September 1939, other service film units, documentaries and newsreels. There was also the vast and varied offer of commercial film production, some of it British in origin, but the majority coming from the enormous US film machine, especially out of Hollywood. It was the Combined Kinematograph Services Film Production and Training Centre – CKS – which produced the *Calling Blighty* films, and it grew out of the Training Film Centre in Bombay, which was making training and education films predominantly for the Indian Army. There were connections with the similarly named AKS, for example, the AKS sent a crew down from its base in Wembley to film the short lived 'answer' message films from relatives in the United Kingdom speaking to their husbands and boyfriends abroad; *A Letter From Home*. These films were said to have been made in factories in the United Kingdom but none have survived (Sargent 1992: 30).

The AKS itself had been established in 1941 by the British government to meet the increasing training and recreational needs of the military services at war. They commissioned up to 150 films a year in wartime (Spicer 2014: 106) and became known as a training ground for a new generation of film directors, cameramen and other talents, many of whom went on post-war to greater success. The novelist Eric Ambler, cinematographers Freddie Francis who much later shot *The Elephant Man*, and Freddie Young who worked on many of David Lean's pictures, the director Carol Reed (*The Third Man*), and actor Peter Ustinov all made their mark in the post-war civilian film world having started in the AKS. Many of the *Calling Blighty* film crew also went on to careers in the film industry, for example, Jack Atcheler who was the camera operator on many noted British productions including *Billy Liar* (1963) and both of the Beatles films. When he was made Head of the AKS, Thorold Dickinson started recruiting talent; he had made his name with his involvement in a highly successful propaganda film commissioned by the War Office and made at Ealing Studios, *The Next of Kin* (1942), which warned against the dangers of careless talk ('Be like dad, keep mum'). The AKS films produced covered a wide variety of styles and subjects, which included food in the mess (*The Soldier's Food* 1942), problems faced by new recruits, and more straightforward technical films on subjects such as how to operate a six-pounder gun and specialized medical films.

In addition to the AKS, the Crown Film Unit produced both feature length and shorter documentary films, and some of these contributed to the pre-eminent reputation of British documentary in wartime. Under the auspices of the Ministry of Information (MOI), the unit produced over 1800 propaganda shorts during the war, with a wide range and variety, as well as the longer and more prestigious documentaries such as *Target For Tonight* (1941), *Western Approaches* (1944) and the seminal Humphrey Jennings film *Fires Were Started* (1943). As Neil Rattigan points out in *This Is England* (2001: 27), most national histories define British wartime film from a rather limited group of high-quality films. As well as the Crown Film Unit pictures, these also include the story documentaries, including *In Which We Serve* (1942), Dickinson's *The Next of Kin* (1942), *The Way Ahead* (1944) – based on the AKS film *The New Lot*, about new recruits – and *We Dive at Dawn* (1943). There had been morale building documentaries focussing on military success, including the popular *Desert Victory* (1942), and *The Way*

Ahead was judged an effective way of countering antagonism in the army, to the extent of being used in Sandhurst post-war as an officer training film (Mackenzie 2001: 125). But significantly absent from this canon were any films about the war in Burma or the Far East. It was only when *Burma Victory* was released in September 1945, after the war had already ended, that the first full-length British film about the Burma campaign appeared.

In fact the most popular British star from 1938 to 1943 was Lancastrian George Formby, and his broad wartime comedy musical of 1940, *Let George Do It*, was one of the most successful films of the year, outgrossing the lauded (John Ford won the Oscar for best director) Hollywood film *The Grapes of Wrath* (1940) in its first month of release. Other home-grown wartime films that were extremely popular at that time but have received little critical attention since, include the Old Mother Riley series of films, based on the musical character played by Arthur Lucan in drag, as an exaggerated Irish working-class woman; seven films were produced during the war in all and found large audiences. The wireless was also very popular as home entertainment, and such broad comedies as *It's That Man Again* with its numerous catchphrases drew in millions of listeners, but widespread television viewing was some ten years in the future, and despite the strictures of wartime, a visit to the cinema, often weekly, was a democratic and compulsive experience for the bulk of the nation. And although British society was ridden by class divisions that were only just beginning to loosen, cinema was enjoyed by all classes, even if the films produced in Britain still reflected social and cultural defining structures.

In 1939, cinemagoing was the most intrinsic social habit of the age and seems to have had positive effects in itself on wartime morale. Cinemas were often extravagant art deco palaces of neon and chrome, large super cinema destination buildings that could accommodate huge audiences, such as the 2300 seater Regent Cinema in Sheffield or the Savoy in Northampton, both of which showed *Calling Blighty* films as well as their usual entertainment programme. The peripheral entertainments of the cinema organ and uniformed usherettes were still common, and there were multiple cinema spaces in even small towns; Bolton had 18 cinemas for a population of 180,000 in the 1930s, and Dundee with only a slightly greater population boasted no less than 28 cinemas. At the advent of war, there were 19 million tickets sold each week and cinema attendance benefited from the paucity of other community entertainment options outside the home; professional cricket and football leagues, for example, were suspended for much of wartime Britain (Farmer 2016: 10–11). Blackouts announced at the outset of hostilities had a brief but dampening effect on cinema attendance, but despite dire predictions that business would be crippled, people did gradually adjust, and viewing picked up and accelerated during the war. By 1945, average weekly cinema admissions had increased significantly; in retrospect, it was the golden age of film as mass popular entertainment. However, this was despite the slump in homegrown film production; domestic fiction film production averaged just 69 films a year in wartime and much of the cinema offering was from the United States (Aldgate and Richards 1986: 2).

Mirroring what would become TV news, the cinema newsreel was a twice-weekly compendium of visual news stories that also covered a wide range of subjects and which had a crossover with the *Calling Blighty* films. Practically every one of Britain's 4500 cinemas showed newsreels, and there were also some dedicated continuously looping news cinemas, which also screened cartoons and travel films, often in the centre of the larger British cities but mostly in London. A dedicated cinemagoer might attend twice a week, so two editions were issued weekly, on Mondays and Thursdays; as film took time to develop, print and edit, the stories were often a little out of date and already known about by a public who read the papers. Burma featured in the reels particularly through the efforts of the cameraman Alec Tozer who filmed the retreat through Burma and its subsequent conquest. As previously noted, Pathé showed as newsreels some films from the invasion of Italy in 1944 titled *Calling Blighty*, which were unrelated to the CKS India/Burma films but had a similar format. These were men talking to their families but they were mixed, from all over the United Kingdom, and were aimed at a general newsreel audience rather than a specific group of relatives. The same films were shared by different newsreel companies so that the same footage appears in a Gaumont-British newsreel about the Allied invasion of Anzio, preceded by generalized shots of the beachhead and under the title *Messages from the Army in Italy* (1944).

There were five newsreel companies in the United Kingdom, which included in addition to the ones mentioned also British Movietone News, British Paramount News and Universal News. When BBC television started again after the war, it also had a bi-weekly news program, but it was, in essence, identical to the cinema newsreels, unlike TV news today (McKernan 2019: n.pag.). The same kinds of synchronized sound on film cameras were used by newsreel crews as in the *Calling Blighty* films but supplemented for the newsreels by silent footage intended for voice over. However, the commentator, often a well-recognized voice such as Leslie Mitchell at Movietone, played the major part in delivering the message for the audience and not unscripted interviews. Like newsreels, the *Blighty* films were often shown as shorts before a main feature, they would have some propaganda value even when a general audience had no specific connection to the men depicted.

Thus in Hull on the 23rd of January 1945 at the Regal Cinema 'relatives of Hull men in India heard and saw them on the screen in the supporting feature *Calling Blighty*'. The main feature was coincidentally related to the war in the Far East, the 1944 film *Dragon Seed*, starring Katharine Hepburn as a (racially miscast) young Chinese wife in a large peasant family resisting the Japanese invasion of China, based on the novel by American Pearl S. Buck, who had spent 30 years in China as the daughter of missionaries. Jade (Hepburn) stands up to the cruel Japanese invaders in the 1930s convincing the more acquiescent village men to offer a strong united front against them. It was anti-Japanese propaganda, with Hollywood actors playing the main Chinese roles (and Chinese actors playing many of the Japanese Invaders), but it was also a rare example of any commercial film that dealt with the Far East war, particularly the Sino-Japanese conflict that predated the incursion into Burma. But not all features had any connection with the *Blighty* shorts that preceded them, so that the Ritz in Belfast showed a *Calling Blighty* film supporting *Waltz Time* 1945, a piece of froth about a young Grand Duchess prevented from marrying the man she loves in imperial Vienna (Belfast Telegraph 1945: 3). And at the Savoy Cinema Northampton in the same year, a *Blighty* film that still survives of 'Northamptonshire men stationed in India' was screened before the 'baffling mystery', *Grand Central Murder* (1942) with Van Heflin, but the film was also screened as a short the same week ahead of Spencer Tracy's *Thirty Seconds Over Tokyo* (1944), which had some relevance as the film depicted the first US bombing raid against Japan in 1942.

It is illuminating to look at what else was showing in one regional city, Liverpool, and surrounding cinemas the same day in summer 1944 that a *Calling Blighty* film of Liverpool men supported *The Lodger* starring Merle Oberon and George Sanders at the art deco Curzon on Prescot Road, which had been built in 1936 and only demolished in 2015. Of an astonishing 98 cinemas in the Greater Liverpool area, nearly all of them were showing escapist Hollywood entertainment. At least four were still screening *Gone With The Wind*, released six years earlier, although the Wintergardens Hoylake hoped to attract flagging audiences by presenting it 'in its entirety at reduced prices'. Comedies such as the Crosby/Hope vehicle *The Road to Singapore* (1940) were popular; *Now Voyager* (1942) with Bette Davis and *The Voice of Terror* (1942) with Basil Rathbone drew the crowds this year, at the height of British cinemagoing, and the city centre Futurist cinema advertized the forthcoming *For Whom the Bell Tolls*. There were few British films and equally rare were war films although the Picturehouse was showing *Wings over the Pacific* and the Savoy, *Guadalcanal Diary* (both 1943), which were also both US viewpoints on the war. Only the Arthur Askey comedy *Bees in Paradise* and *Heaven is Round the Corner* (both 1944) with Will Fyfe were UK-originated films to compete with the overwhelming US industrial output. An indication of the public's current taste could be hinted at with the Rialto and Hippodrome's description of the Will Fyfe film as 'a romantic musical story that has *nothing to do with the war*' (Liverpool Evening Express 1944: 2).

None of the films on offer in Liverpool that Wednesday in 1944 were documentaries, despite the commonly held view that World War II represented the apogee of British documentary, at least up to that point. Many of the iconic documentary films of the period, *Fires Were Started* (1943), *Listen To Britain* (1942), *A Diary For Timothy* (1945), were by Humphrey Jennings, who had co-founded the Mass Observation movement in 1937 and who pioneered the use of 'real' subjects in his films, albeit playing themselves in a story-documentary format. Some of these films presented their real subjects with a degree of informality but within a scripted structure; for example, *Fires Were Started*, about firemen in the Blitz, where as Brian Winston noted Jennings had by 1942 developed a method of coaxing a kind of naturalness from his non-actor subjects, mainly by using multiple takes that 'rendered an exhausted performer far more relaxed and less camera conscious' (Smith 2003: 138). However, this was far from a fly on the wall documentary, being a highly constructed narrative, where the interiors were shot at Pinewood Studios. Jennings had to contend with a natural British understated reserve that he overcame in his protagonists, played by real firemen but these were far from informal or self-authored statements, and were also far from the *Blighty* approach where men delivered their own messages, within their largely self-imposed format.

One of the issues that British documentarists failed to grapple with was that they were largely themselves drawn from the upper middle classes, and whilst they approved in a patrician way of the portrayal of the nobility of the working classes, this did not extend to the idea of giving them an unmediated voice. As previously noted, the 1935 film *Housing Problems* was the first in which working-class voices were heard, but they come across awkwardly, with little naturalness. However, this was a huge advance over what had come before; as Grierson claimed, 'Remember there were no working class on the screen when I started out. I was the first guy to put the working class on screen believe it or not' (Sussex 1975: 194). In the early 1930s, the attitude as expressed in the films was that 'work in itself is ennobling, and hence it is no part of the general purpose to get too close to working people as people, to reveal their pay or living conditions' (Sussex 1975: 42). The workingman had to be heroic as Anstey had remarked, and *Housing Problems* was a step forward as Arthur Elton who collaborated on it maintained: '[it was] like a television presentation, only long before television'. However, a lot of credit for this is said to be Ruby Grierson's, who assisted on the film and had an ability to win confidence that gave the subjects a relative spontaneity in the interviews. The idea of even appearing in a film was so alien that one woman who appeared in it according to Anstey did not recognize herself, even after the film was shown to her twice; in middle age, she had never been to the centre of London from Stepney (Sussex 1975: 63). It was only eight years later that the *Calling Blighty* films came to be made, but the attitudes towards film and depiction of ordinary people in the film had not changed hugely.

In a way this approach to workers and incidentally to the variety of regional accents in Britain (Housing Problems was very much a London film) was anachronistic. The Lumiere brothers had shown workers leaving their photographic factory in Lyon, flooding through the factory gates in 1895, in what is often referred to as the first real motion picture ever made, but of course there was no sound, and the workers were not delineated as individuals. Also missing in the documentaries of the 1930s and 1940s was spontaneity. In the Ministry of Information short *Shunter Black's Night Off*, written and directed by Max Munden in 1941, 'based on a true story', the film is narrated by the railway worker Joe Black, but actually wholly scripted by Munden, with the protagonist played by an unnamed actor (actually John Slater). The film *Ordinary People* of the same year was preceded by an opening title 'To the Future historian – THIS FILM WAS PLAYED BY ORDINARY PEOPLE OF LONDON'; however, it was an enacted reconstruction. This was typical of wartime output; in *Western Approaches* 1944 made by Pat Jackson for the Crown Film Unit, about the battle of the Atlantic, real seamen recruited in a Liverpool pub played the crew of a lifeboat, but the dialogue was completely scripted. It was either learnt word for word by the amateur cast or in one case by a man called Banner put into his own words, which was gradually also adopted by some of the seamen (Sussex 1975: 149). This story documentary, what today would be called docufiction, was innovative and unusual in that it was shot in Technicolor, but in its occasional performative awkwardness, it was far from off the cuff.

The *Blighty* films, within the simple message format, framed by military protocol, represented authenticity on screen at a time when this did not exist. Partly the technology to make this possible had emerged only relatively recently, but also the war and a morale-building imperative bypassed the unwritten rules of propaganda and documentary, to connect to the voices of the United Kingdom. The role of the everyman, of the average hero, was replaced by individuals, who came into focus in these masculine wartime expressions. Jo Fox identifies that at this time 'The use of accents and language was one of the most important devices in the formation of both the collective experience and individual identities' (Fox 2006: 820). The success of George Formby in wartime and to some extent Gracie Fields, despite their thick Lancashire accents seemed to appeal to a public who wanted the little man (or woman) to win through against the odds, and on the BBC the soft Halifax accent of Wilfred Pickles was also extremely popular. Pickles was even the first regional voice to be heard on radio, if only occasionally, as a newsreader during World War II, allegedly as a 'move to make it more difficult for Nazis to impersonate BBC broadcasters' (BBC Voices Your Voice 2014: n.pag.).

But the trade journal *Documentary News* still critically noted in 1941 that the West-end manner embodied in film only admirable human qualities and 'working class and dialect speaking characters are conventionally endowed with comic or criminal traits' (Fox 2006: 829). Humphrey Jennings's *Target For Tonight* (1941) deliberately included dialogue and accents to show individual identities working together, including broad Scots and Canadian dialect, but within of course scripted dialogue, and the treatment for Fires Were Started carefully detailed varied accents, from cockney to Liverpool Irish. However, even Jennings 'omitted the foul language that was in everybody's mouth at the time' (Smith 2003: 138). Nor for obvious reasons was there any 'foul' language in the *Blighty* films, despite the odd sexual innuendo, although one man does swear in one of the remaining films when he forgets what to say, and the soundtrack is muted completely at that point (*CB* 132 1945).

Feature films such as *In Which We Serve* (1943) drew inspiration from documentary, and accent and class were faced in the fictional narrative *Millions Like Us* (1943) where the society girl Jennifer and the factory foreman Charlie are driven apart by social barriers. But in *Mrs Miniver* (1942), the Hollywood view of British society reverted to class clichés, the maid depicted as a 'giggling half-wit' (Fox 2006: 837). However, as the snapshot of Liverpool filmgoing in 1944 indicates, as the war rolled on the overwhelming desire was for escapism and the perceived classless status of the American accent. This is underscored by the *Blighty* films where, in comparing their performances ironically to screen actors, the ones mentioned are nearly all from the United States; Don Ameche, Mickey Mouse or Jimmy Durante. However, almost absent in any of the wartime output either in the United States or the United Kingdom was any depiction in either fiction or documentary of the military efforts in the war in the Far East.

The Forgotten Army was equally forgotten in film during wartime; the major Allied effort that involved more than a million men received much less exposure than the campaigns in Africa or North West Europe. Although covered in newsreels, mostly from a propaganda point of view, and the occasional MOI short such as the ten-minute *Central Front Burma* 1945, the three major films on the Far East campaign, *Burma Victory*, *The Stilwell Road* and *Objective Burma*, were not released in the United Kingdom until 1945 after the war was over and were mired in controversy. In particular, there was a clash of focus over the differing aims of the United States and British government forces in the war. During wartime, a small number of Hollywood features dealt with Burma, in a rather myopic or trivial way. *Rookies in Burma* (1943), for example, was a 'fast and furious comedy filled with the sort of humour that appeals strongly to the unsophisticated' (*Film Daily* 1943: 12).

In it, two GI privates assigned to kitchen duty end up in a Japanese prisoner of war camp but escape after improbably overpowering their Japanese guards. 1942's *A Yank on the Burma Road* (aka *China Caravan*) was about a New York cabbie who equally improbably ends up leading a caravan of medical supplies to Chungking; a pre-Ledo Road piece of propaganda mixed with a love story that focused on the US's Chinese allies. In *Bombs Over Burma* (1942), the construction of a supply road very like the Ledo Road is even sabotaged by an ostensible British ally, an English nobleman, who turns out to be a German agent. There was also at least one Indian film about the Burma campaign, produced under an Indian government edict of 1943 that out of every three Indian films made, at least one should be a war-effort film supporting the British position. *Burma Rani* (1945) was a Tamil language film about a supposed British spy ring in occupied Rangoon led by a Tamil woman, which tried to answer the Japanese propaganda expressed in the film by a Japanese general, that 'Asia is for Asians'. In terms of the amount of screen hours, apart from newsreels, the eighty or more hours of *Calling Blighty* films dwarfed in output the commercial cinema that dealt with Burma between 1944 and 1946 by many times.

The first major Burma film that was screened in Britain in September 1945 was highly controversial, and after a week's exhibition in the West End, was banned from public showing and not screened again until 1952, when it was shown with a new prologue and to much sarcasm in the press. *Objective Burma* (1945) was a Hollywood film starring Errol Flynn, which attracted a storm of protest from British newspapers for suggesting that Burma had been liberated by the Americans, ignoring the efforts of General Slim's 14th army. There was some justification in the claim although the fact that it was the first to reach the British cinemagoing public about the war in Burma might have particularly inflamed popular opinion. When the subsequent *Burma Victory* was previewed to the press in the same month, September 1945, the *Aberdeen Press and Journal* special correspondent saw it as 'Britain's answer to Hollywood's film travesty', which gave 'full credit to the Fourteenth Army and all the other allied forces that featured in the campaign' (*Aberdeen Press and Journal* 1945: n.pag.). Actually, that film was equally a partial and British view of the conflict, considered by film historian Ian Jarvie in terms of its authenticity on historical matters in the war in Burma as 'worse than useless' (along with *Objective Burma* and *The Stillwell Road*) (Jarvie 1988: 68). *Objective Burma* was a Hollywood account of an expedition behind Japanese lines to destroy a radar installation and was very loosely based on the exploits of Merrill's Marauders, the US counterpart to the Chindits. It had a preliminary title mentioning the involvement of British, Indian and Chinese troops; however, most of the film was an adventure yarn, skilfully directed by Raoul Walsh, and shot by the acclaimed cinematographer James Wong Howe. Despite its reception in the

United Kingdom, it was Warner Brothers' sixth most popular film that year and it also did very well in France. Errol Flynn's performance was relatively understated and it was called (in the United States) 'one of the best war films made in Hollywood' (*New York Times* 1945: 10).

The other film, *Burma Victory* (1945) with a much more British point of view, was in post-production at the time, but this also had been riven by dissent, albeit behind the scenes. The film was conceived in 1944 by Mountbatten, Head of South East Asia Command, as a joint full-length production, British and American, which would tell the full story of SEAC in the Far East and Burma in particular. The problem was that whilst the British intended to stress the fight against the Japanese and downplay any colonial implications, the Americans were mostly concerned with the Ledo Road as a road bridge to China to support their Chinese allies and were against any portrayal that seemed to show them supporting the British Empire. The proposed film fell apart in acrimony and turned into two films sharing the same source material; *Burma Victory*, made in the United Kingdom and *The Stilwell Road* in the United States (Osborne 2010: n.pag.). Whilst incorporating newsreel and SEAC film, *Burma Victory* uses the fictional device of one soldier's diaries to embody the narrative, along with maps and combat footage (and is in that sense similar to the much later TV Channel 4 *Messages Home* programme, about the *Calling Blighty* films, where the stories of individual soldiers were used to piece together the campaign as a whole). Burma, and particularly the Burmese monsoon, is seen as a dystopian anti-paradise, almost equalling the Japanese enemy, which has echoes in the *Blighty* films where in contrast to scenes on leave on the beach at Malabar Bay, Bombay, the soldiers' comments sometimes echo an alienation from their surroundings. The film begins with a soldier reading out a colourful description of the country from a tourist brochure: 'Burma, there is romance in the very word'. After descriptions of the pagodas and the light-hearted people, the reader exclaims 'would you believe it!', as the camera pans to a sodden forest in the monsoon downpour. The film was warmly praised in both countries, for its 'convincing authenticity, and in its story of the unimaginable terrors of the jungle' (Motion Picture Herald 1945: 46).

The Stilwell Road focused on the construction of the Ledo Road under US General Joseph Stilwell (after whom the road was later renamed). Narrated by Ronald Reagan, it showed the three-year project undertaken by 15,000 soldiers and 35,000 predominantly Chinese volunteers (Osborne 2009: n.pag.) and was ironically, given it was a US film, probably more inclusive of the other nationalities in the war and more detailed in its chronology of the allied manoeuvres than *Burma Victory*. In addition, the US film discloses its use of reconstructed footage, whereas Burma victory disguises its staged scenes filmed at Pinewood Studios (Colonial Film Burma Victory 2010). Ultimately, as *The Stilwell Road* was withdrawn by the military in the United States and not shown commercially, whereas *Burma Victory* was distributed there by Warner Brothers (who coincidentally also produced *Objective Burma*), it was the latter that was much more successful. This was despite its weaknesses, such as some unconvincingly restaged conferences featuring Mountbatten and other military leaders, which Mountbatten unsuccessfully tried too late to have removed from director Roy Boulting's final cut.

After the three Burma films, one of which was hardly seen in the United Kingdom, one was withdrawn and only *Burma Victory* widely distributed, for the next decade almost no commercial films made anywhere dealt with the 14th Army or the Burma campaign; those few that can be loosely grouped as dealing with this theme are concerned with failure and compromise. *The Bridge over the River Kwai* (1957) and *King Rat* (1965), for example, are about Allied prisoners of war (as is the more recent *Merry Christmas Mr Lawrence*, 1983, set in Java). *Yesterday's Enemy* (1959) is reportedly based on a war crime perpetrated by a British army captain in Burma in 1942. The film questions military values and depicts British soldiers threatening to shoot Burmese hostages if an informer does not co-operate, then at the end they all face a Japanese firing squad (Mackenzie 2001: 135). This dystopian and anti-heroic view of the war contrasts acutely with other post-war fictional films of heroism and victory, such as *The Dam Busters* (1955), *Ice Cold in Alex* (1958) or even the understated *The Cruel Sea* (1953). A later film based on Willis Hall's stage play, *The Long and the Short and the Tall* (1961) continued the downbeat tone with its narrative about a squabbling British unit in 1942 in Burma, who capture and then kill a Japanese soldier, and then are almost all killed themselves. This is very far from the derring-do of *Objective Burma*, and the dominant image of the Burma war that has emerged on-screen in the decades after it ended is one of moral doubt and defeat.

The Indian nationalist point of view is seldom represented in film, but the 2017 Bollywood musical *Rangoon* is unusual in supporting the Indian National Army and representing the British as arrogant and as much the enemy as the Japanese. The film ends with a company of British troops massacred on a bridge, the resident British commander beheaded by the Indian hero, and an end title proclaiming the INA raising the Indian flag in 1944. Ironically, it is in a Japanese film, *The Burmese Harp* [*Biruma no Tategoto*] (1956), which won the following year's Academy Award for the best foreign-language film, that the war is embodied by images of redemption and even unity between cultural groups. The film concerns Private Mizushima, a musician and harp player in a Japanese company, who tries to convince his countrymen to surrender when he learns the war is over, but they refuse, he is beaten, and then all the others die in a bombardment. Mizushima recovers and devotes his time in Burma to burying Japanese corpses he finds on a solitary pilgrimage, and after first impersonating a Buddhist monk, he starts to study Buddhism seriously and refuses to return to Japan. In an early scene, his company realizes that they are being watched by Indian and British soldiers, and as they sing in Japanese, they are joined by the enemy troops singing the same tune, 'Home Sweet Home'. Burma is also shown in the film, not as an alien dystopia, but rather possessing an 'eerie power' in its landscape, Buddhist statuary and architecture (Bock 1993: n.pag.).

The *Calling Blighty* films were part of wartime cinema concerning Burma and the Far East war but stand apart from it. They were made in a pre-television age during the golden epoch of cinemagoing, using heavy and expensive technology that seems to belong to a different world to smartphones, YouTube and a contemporary awareness of self-presentation on screen. They have a simplicity in their message, a keep-your-chins-up, keep-smiling positivity that belies the horrors of the war in Burma and the complex range of positions that were represented in films about the conflict. In their cross-section of men from across the United Kingdom, and the sheer amount of film produced, plus the self-authored content, they take their place among wartime film output, not documentary or fiction but a unique document that goes beneath the surface of the prevailing representation of men on screen to preserve an authenticity unknown at the time.

3

Living Letters:
How the Films Came About

We must again resign ourselves to spend this, our fourth Christmas, in this so-called 'mystic land of the East' where only filth, poverty and desolation reign supreme.

(Soldier's letter to the *Worthing Herald* in 1945
[Parr 1945: n.pag.])

It was the sense of invisibility cloaking the British servicemen in the 14th Army and the lack of morale that that engendered, that essentially gave rise to the *Calling Blighty* films, although there were multiple antecedents in different forms of communication, especially letters from men serving in war. How the films practically came about on the other hand had been contested but has become much clearer. For soldiers engaged in a long war and who are distant from their homeland, contact with parents, wives, sweethearts and children has always been of vital importance, and for centuries, the principal way of communicating with them has been the written letter. Soldiers' letters exist in the Imperial War Museum from the American Civil War and even earlier, and by World War I, over 19,000 mailbags were crossing the channel each day with letters to and from the men at the front (Mason et al. 2018: n.pag.)

The other channel of communication in a pre-electronic messaging era was that of home leave, but whilst this was possible for men serving in the European theatre, the distances were so great to the Far East and the availability of transport so limited that the possibility of leave was in practice negligible. As seen in Louis Schimberg's *Blighty* message, he had been away from his family for over six years, and his experience was not unusual. It is over four and a half thousand miles from Bombay to London, and a further thousand miles to Rangoon. It took Tag Barnes 31 days to sail to Bombay from Liverpool, but with the inevitable army and navy delays on route, and the long journey across India on the unreliable railway system, the whole trip could take months. The average tour of duty served by the ordinary soldier overseas was six years if they enlisted at the outset, reduced by mid-1945 to three years four months for those serving in SEAC. The RAF served three years and the Navy two years. The US servicemen usually served two years, but sometimes only six months, and the average overseas tour was 16 months, which led to a further sense of discrimination for the British soldiers compared to the Americans (Sparrow 1949: 9).

Morale is at the heart of the need to better connect soldiers with their families. The conditions of combat or even training in India were extraordinarily debilitating for the British soldier (and incidentally for the Japanese alike). The extreme heat, the monsoon rains that meant staying wet for months on end, and the especially difficult nature of the terrain, which entailed long treks up and down steep and jungle-clad hills to move even short distances, all depressed the spirits of the British forces unused to tropical warfare. Letters to and from Blighty were a lifeline, but the surface post took a long time to transport and airmail was restricted until at least December 1944. 'Airmail' went only partly by air, and letters were restricted to eight per month for each individual; the scarcity of air transport resulted often in the aerograms taking almost as long as the free 'on active Service' surface mail (Sargent 1992: 1). In James Fenton's collected letters from Burma, *The Forgotten Army* (2012: 55), he comments about the many airgraphs he sent home, that they were letters 10″ × 8″ in size, specially printed to streamline written communication with relatives back in the United Kingdom. The letters were copied onto microfilm and forwarded in bulk to print smaller and then folded and sealed with the address visible – the message had to be written within the borders of a single sheet of paper. One airgraph was issued each week to personnel serving overseas from 1941 until it was discontinued on 31 July 1945. For Fenton in India, the air letter cards and airgraphs took a not inconsiderable 19 days, but ordinary sea mail even longer, about three months. He abandoned sending letters ordinary mail because of the extreme delays in getting news to and fro (Fenton 2012: 67).

Fenton's frequent references to the mail reflect the preoccupation of the men in the *Blighty* films. Men got a free blue airmail letter and card weekly but if two envelopes were sent by one person, the second went by slow surface mail. Letters the other way round did not always go by air even with a blue label and two shillings worth of stamps (Fenton 2012: 73). When in action the mail was even slower: 'I may not be able to write frequently because of the remote postal service, the censoring of letters, or the availability of postage stamps'. The physical conditions of writing could also be difficult: 'You cannot fail to notice my writing as a little bit better after removing a load of sand from the nib'. The ink also dried out in the heat (Fenton 2012: 95). Even telegrams for urgent news took time to arrive; they were quickly received in Calcutta but took another week to two weeks to get to the isolated jungles of Burma . There was also an EFM, a special telegram that made for easy transmission, as three separate phrases were selected from a printed list, where each phrase had a specific code number. Fenton notes his surprise when he was told by the telegraph operator that a new phrase had been added to the list – 'I am expecting a baby'. The importance of sending letters to men in the Far East was even emphasized in a Ministry of Information short animated film, *Writing's Worthwhile* (1945), which had helpful hints on what to include, family news mostly, which would it said be with him in a (rather optimistic) five days.

There were other factors that emphasized the isolation. The social centres of the Navy, Army and Air Force Institutes, the NAAFIs dispensing tea and bottled beer to the troops through clouds of cigarette smoke were few and far between or sometimes non-existent. The purported NAAFI canteen in which most of the *Calling Blighty* films were made was constructed in a film studio and was regarded as a fantasy version of the real thing by the men in the films. According to the *Basra Times* in 1944, this even caused protests in Britain when the truth leaked out. 'A recently screened War Office experiment film has caused a storm among relatives who faced cameras and gave messages to folk at home from a "typical canteen". Wives and sweethearts were still discussing the "lovely canteen" when letters from the troops arrived telling them that palatial canteen was in fact a film set' (Basra Times 1944: n.pag.).

But also wireless sets, cinemas and visits by entertainers of the Entertainments National Service Association (ENSA) were also restricted or completely absent. In one *Calling Blighty* film, a special point is made of filming a group

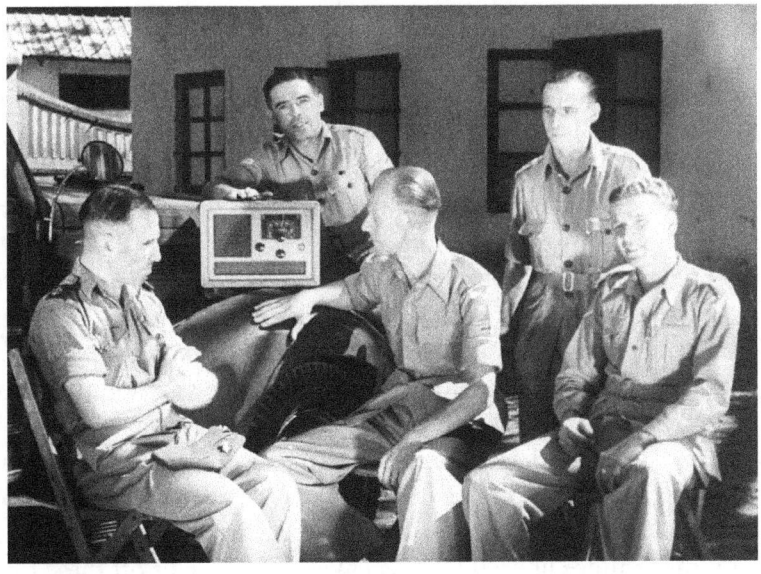

FIGURE 3.1: Men deliver messages from Bombay with prominent radio set (*CB* 273 1946). © IWM.

of Manchester men clustered around a large radio set, which is playing Indian music, which one of the men switches off before he delivers his message. It remains prominent in the shot as the soldiers all speak, but this was a deliberate construction meant to impress relatives thousands of miles away, rather than a substantial truth. ENSA performers (it was popularly held to mean Every Night Something Awful) did visit Burma and India, but the physical discomfort of the tropics could not have made it a very popular posting. George Formby and Vera Lynn were highly regarded for performing for the 14th Army, and other acts such as the cockney gossiping duo Gert and Daisy were a great hit. Even Noel Coward, a personal friend of Mountbatten, also gave concerts to mixed reactions. Coward gave performances for the US troops, predominantly African-American who were constructing the Ledo Road in Burma, the 1000 mile long road between India and China, but they had never heard of the 'Limey piano tinkler', failed to respond to his sophisticated cabaret, and gave him the slow handclap, and Coward was also unhappy at having to sing as lorries and heavy transports rumbled past on the road beside him (Allen 1984: 363). However, Coward's broadcast on the Home Service on his return in 1944 about the Forgotten Army, a personal pledge to Mountbatten, led to congratulations from the King and 2000 letters of support. He denounced the press for ignoring the men, explained the terrible conditions they served under and praised their indomitable courage (Aldgate and Richards 1986: 193).

These visitors were in any case rare exceptions. In Tag Barnes's account of his service in India and Burma, there are no ENSA performances mentioned, although he does see Noel Coward in the street outside Bombay Town Hall (Barnes 1991: 65). He has infrequent opportunities to see films in India, and even one in Burma at Christmas 1944, although the experience was disappointing. 'A film was shown in the canteen called *This Is the Army* (the Warner Brothers film of Irving Berlin's wartime stage show). It was spoiled somewhat because there was only one projector and every 15 minutes the show was stopped while a new reel was fitted' (Barnes 1991: 84).

Even beer, if it could be obtained at all, was severely limited and restricted to one bottle of month – the troops called it 'the monthly insult' (Sargent 1992: n.pag.). This is much commented upon by the men in the *Calling Blighty* films: 'There's been no beer at all. I've not had a drink since Christmas, see what you can do about that down there' (*CB* 203 1945). There was a sense that the British soldier was at a severe disadvantage in terms of home comforts compared to US troops who were serving in the same conflict. The US soldiers had unlimited supplies of tinned beer, ice cream and Coca-Cola, whereas the British Tommy had to survive on much more limited rations. 'We're keeping fit off these tins of Irish stew, bully beef, biscuits, little bits of chocolate thrown in now and again' (*CB* 212 1945) one Manchester soldier tells his family from a location in Burma. One

American camp near the Myitkyina airstrip even had the unimaginable luxury of air conditioning (Fox 2013: 43).

There was even a possibility that such disaffection would potentially give rise to mutiny although Mountbatten himself and other senior officers discounted the risk of this. A report by the Earl of Münster published in November 1944 after a fact-finding mission on a tour of South East Asia Command, set out the men's many grievances and laid bare their disquiet about welfare. And although following VE Day, there was widespread demobilisation of the troops serving in the United Kingdom and Europe, in the Far East, demob proceeded much more slowly, partly due to the shortage of ships and other transport. Hence the *Calling Blighty* films continued well into 1946, nearly a year after the war had ended. The dissatisfaction of the 14th Army soldiers stuck out in Malaya after the Japanese had surrendered was put into words by one local man in Worthing, E.A. Parr of the Royal Sussex Regiment, who wrote to his local paper the Herald in October 1945. They were 'serving in Malaya as an army of occupation – to my mind their unjust reward for fifteen months of action in two campaigns i.e. Arakan and extreme North Burma. Both the actions took place in indescribable country and conditions'. He lamented the industrial action then taking place in Britain – 'It is with horror that we read of the despicable and contemptible conduct of the dockers and stevedores in striking at such an inopportune moment', and regretted that their hopes of being home by Christmas would be dashed (Parr 1945: n.pag.).

It was against this background of poor morale and desperate conditions that the *Calling Blighty* film series came into being, facilitated by the technological developments that had emerged since World War I. Radio and the development of the gramophone record had opened up new possibilities of voice communication, but it was the development of sound on film in the 1930s that gave special impetus to the *Blighty* message films. The direct forerunner of the films was the Forces Programme and associated short wave services that used radio as the most efficient medium to reach the troops across several theatres of war. A broadcasting section was set up in the welfare directorate of the services in the summer of 1942, to liaise with the BBC, and in 1943 plans were laid for such features as the War Office originated '*Calling The Army*' where war office personalities were interviewed by members of the forces to discuss army questions of special interest to the troops (Crang 2000: 97). The Army also developed its own broadcasting facilities overseas and produced features in India for the troops, run by Major Cave-Brown Cave, a former BBC producer. An important and popular initiative of forces broadcasting was the compilation of message programmes, such as *Cairo Calling*, where from 1943 radio messages for Middle East Forces, from Iraq, Transjordan, Syria and Palestine, were recorded by members of the services for their relatives and friends in Great Britain, introduced by Peter Haddon. A film recreation of how these messages were received was made by Pathé with actors portraying the unlucky family whose son was silent as he had been captured. In the film, *Until the Day* (1943–1945), about Red Cross parcels for PoWs, one soldier gives his message and says prophetically 'I wish this was television so you can see how I am keeping'. This scheme was later extended to greetings from West Africa and India and was the first instance of the *Calling Blighty* title applied to a radio programme, where soldiers recorded audio messages to be broadcast to their families in Britain (Crang 2000: 97). A field broadcasting unit in North-West Europe was set up under Major John McMillan, and when he discovered a direct telephone line from Hamburg to a telephone exchange in Goodge Street London, so was born from November 1943 the very long-running radio programme *Forces Favourites* (later *Two Way Family Favourites*), 'in which music is played at the request of Forces Overseas for their relatives at home', by the BBC's General Overseas Service. This request programme linking servicemen in Germany with families in the United Kingdom, continued until 1984 (Crang 2000: 97).

There were other radio message programmes to lift the spirits of the troops and connect families, incidentally boosting civilian morale; *Hello Parents* linked parents and their evacuee children in Australia and South Africa, and these and other programmes consisted largely of pre-recorded messages by relatives or others read out by the presenter – 'Children have been calling home from the United States and Canada every month since Enid Maxwell inaugurated this radio link between the Old World and the New on Christmas Day. On Boxing Day children "called home" from Australia. Today marks the opening of a regular service, between parents over here and their children "down under"' (*Radio Times* 1941: 18). *Children Calling Home* was, however, a two-way conversation; one was filmed for a Pathé newsreel in 1941 as children in the United States and Canada spoke to their parents in London, but judging by this the experience was stilted in the extreme (*Children Calling Home* 1941). One-way programmes also continued alongside these, and one, *Sincerely Yours Vera Lynn*, devised to improve the morale of servicemen and their wives and sweethearts separated by the war, became one of the BBC's most listened to programmes (Mackay 2003: 104). This included 'News from Home, messages from munitions girls to their husbands and congratulations to some new fathers in the Forces'. The *Radio Times* (1941: 7) explained that the producer's 'great hope is that twins will arrive just before a broadcast, so he has arranged with the London hospitals that they should telephone the BBC any time twins are born there on Sundays. Failing that, he rings one of the hospitals to collect a story about a soldier's baby born during the day'. *Your Family Album* also consisted of messages collected by the army radio units from families of men serving in SEAC and was broadcast to soldiers in India from New Delhi (Sargent 1992: 2).

By 1942, there was a vast network of BBC message programmes connecting forces in various parts of the world with their families, and much of this was two-way traffic. The popular organist Sandy Macpherson had a weekly programme, *Sandy's Half-hour* in which he broadcast messages to and from serving men and women in addition to *Sandy Calling* (to the Middle East) and *Sandy Calling India*. So many greetings were being sent that a standard telegram phrase used to save money became 'Hearing your voice on the wireless gave me such a thrill'. However, the BBC warned that 'with the best will in the world it can only broadcast a fraction of these greetings and requests received'. To avoid disappointment, they discouraged further applications for the Middle East for example, where several thousand were on the waiting list (Birmingham Mail 1942: 8). Nor were these moving images, what would come to be termed '"See Me Hear Me" film snaps' (*Aberdeen Press and Journal* 1943: 4). One film does exist of children evacuated to the United States sending messages home to Britain from a New York studio in 1940, a Reuters-British Paramount newsreel. The messages are obviously spontaneous; when asked whether she is happy in the United States one of the three children says 'fairly', then after encouragement to say something to her folks back home, she adds 'Well, I hope you're not dead yet' (*USA Sevacs tell Mum over radio* 1941).

There were also Army newspapers, especially where civilian newspapers were difficult to obtain in outlying parts of the theatre of war. Provincial newspapers in the United Kingdom ran personal 'name and address' stories but coverage of the Far East was poor, partly because until mid-1944 there was precious little to cheer about except for the sporadic Chindit incursions behind Japanese lines. However, there was also the *South East Asia Command* newspaper, edited by Frank Owen, who had edited the *London Evening Standard*, which provided a welcome focus, but units also began to produce their own newspapers (Sargent 1992: 3). Tag Barnes became the troop editor of a magazine launched by Brigade headquarters in 1944 called 'The Third Jungle Book', his job being to record any interesting or unusual events that occurred in his number six troop. As he laconically comments, 'it added a bit of interest to life' (Barnes 1991: 66). There was even a project to use the gramophone record to create an audio equivalent of the aerograph. For 1/9d, the Voices of the Forces scheme devised by the NAAFI allowed servicemen and women to record up to 180 words on an aluminium disc at specially installed recording booths in NAAFI clubs overseas. The sender could read from a prepared script or choose from a number of stock phrases, and it was said in a newsreel about the initiative that hundreds of discs a day were being flown home; however, this was made in September 1945 after the war was over (*Voices of the Forces* 1945).

The attraction of a message medium where families could see their loved ones and gain reassurance as to their health and well-being as well as hear them, was compelling and the technology to enable this was rapidly advancing in the 1940s. When the seminal film *Housing Problems* was made in 1935, the first documentary film in which the subjects, working people in the East End of London, could be heard and seen on screen speaking in a relatively unscripted way, the sound recording equipment was enormous. It consisted of a 'vast sound truck outside, full of batteries, and a big sound camera. It was terribly cumbersome equipment try and do that stuff with' (Sussex 1975: 63). A sound studio would be needed in order to film soldiers who could be gathered together from different parts of the Far East, a difficult enough feat of organisation itself. But to film men in the field a more portable solution had to be developed. At first sound was recorded on a separate 'camera', which printed the synchronized sound optically on a separate strip of 35mm film, but later in 1945 advances meant that the audio could be recorded on the same film as the pictures, making the equipment much more portable relatively speaking, for filming deep in Burma and Malaya (Abbott 1992: n.pag.).

The idea for the *Calling Blighty* films has been attributed to more than one source. The famous newsreel cameraman Paul Wyand who was later one of the first to film the opening of the Belsen concentration camp, says in his memoir *Useless If Delayed* that in Italy covering the Allied landings, things quietened as preparations were made for the assault on Monte Cassino, so he looked around for other stories to cover. Hitting on the idea of recording messages from the troops to their families in Britain, he selected men from the most remote parts he could find and grouped them by a particular area, to start with servicemen from Liverpool and Glasgow (Wyand 1959: 100). He also says that the Americans asked him to record their troops, but none of these films seem to have survived, and the remaining (Pathé) films from Italy show men from very different regions in the same film. These were newsreel films for British Movietone News rather than official army productions, and the interviews were first included in a Movietone newsreel issued in the United Kingdom on the 10th of February 1944 under the title *Messages Home*. Due to the success of the newsreels, he was soon asked to interview men from cities that Movietone chose themselves. His extensive equipment, which had been allocated to him as an experiment in November 1943, just about fitted into a large Humber Imperial car; it included his big sound camera that weighed a hundredweight, a silent combat camera, 20,000 feet of film and five hundredweight of batteries and assorted sound equipment (Wyand 1959: 92). Under the rota system, news stories were shared and passed on via the Ministry of information and so two other newsreel companies, Gaumont British News and Pathé Gazette released the film on the same day, Pathé calling it *Calling Blighty*.

However, the first *Calling Blighty* film from India had in fact been screened several months earlier in London, on 16 September 1943, and most likely filmed in summer 1943, so it is likely that Wyand's newsreel films from Italy were a parallel initiative. He was probably unaware of the much larger organisation of the studio filming several thousand miles to the East, which were also very specifically aimed at particular families. The announcer Bob Danvers-Walker mentions at the beginning of what was probably the first of Wyand's newsreels, a Pathé film from Italy 1944 that 'For many months now we have been sending spoken messages from Canadians in Britain to their folks at home. Now here are messages from our boys in Italy to their relations in Britain' (Pathé *Calling Blighty* 1944). Some fragments of the Canadian films exist in the Pathé archives, and they may have originated about the same time as the Far East *Blighty* films but were unrelated and on a much smaller scale, and for a general newsreel audience. They seem to have been from Canadians in London aimed at families in London, Ontario.

Reports in the *Yorkshire Post* give vivid impressions of the first *Calling Bighty* screening from India. 'Relatives of 21 London soldiers now serving in India gathered at the Curzon cinema tonight to both see and hear their loved ones in a ten-minute film, *Calling Blighty*, that has been made by the War Office. Suggested by messages broadcast by the BBC, this film is the first of its kind. The scheme is still in its experimental stages. Judging by the applause accorded it tonight, I do not think the authorities will have any doubts about its success' (*Yorkshire Post and Leeds Intelligencer* 1943: 2). And under the headline 'Look at Bill', the *Liverpool Daily Post* report enthused 'I sat with a cinema audience who would not have exchanged the spectacle before them for the sight of the most glamorous film stars in the world [...] they were London lads out East in this film tonight'. The audience were 'buxom cockney mamas, come out in their best hats, pretty young wives, grey-haired fathers and wriggling little nippers [...]. There would be clapping and happy cries now here, now there. If you put all the cinemas in London together the pleasure they provided tonight would come nowhere near the happiness this ten minute film gave' (*Liverpool Daily Post* 1943: 2).

The newspaper reports make it clear that the films were an extension of the scheme of radio greetings from the troops, the *Calling Blighty* radio programme where the title most probably originated. The second film was screened later in September 1943 in Glasgow at the Scala Cinema to similar acclaim: 'The comments of the parents, who were present on the invitation of the army authorities, showed that it was an unqualified success' (*The Scotsman* 1943: n.pag.). That these first films were said to have been made in a NAAFI canteen by the army film unit, shows that they had been filmed on the film set in Bombay: the location films came later. In February 1944 it was reported that 'plans are in hand at GHQ in India for a mobile film unit to visit forward areas' (*Middlesex Chronicle* 1944: 6). It was said in the same article about cameramen of the Services Film Centre that they had visited canteens in India; the truth that it was a single constructed film set was not yet apparent.

It may be that the messages film was an idea that had sprung up coincidentally in any case in different parts of the world, but as a one-off novelty. The Imperial War Museum holds a newsreel item called *Messages Home* filmed in Australia apparently in 1942. The donor, whose husband Corporal Albert Powell speaks in the film, said that it had been shot in Melbourne after the arrival in Australia of the remnants of two squadrons who had escaped from Singapore on a Dutch steamer in January 1942, and that it had been screened in a Bristol cinema to his mother to show that he was still alive and not missing in action as was believed. In it, the well-known voice of newsreels Bob Danvers-Walker makes the variety of regional accents of the men a source of humour, quite unlike the natural acceptance of British accents found in the later film series. 'It's an accepted fact that they're from all parts of the British Isles'; men then variously speak in Scottish, Irish, Welsh (Taffy from Glamorgan, South Wales), London, Geordie and other accents and talk of missing Yorkshire pudding or Lancashire hotpot (*Messages Home* 1942).

The idea for the films it has been suggested came from Major Stephen McCormack, who was a key organizer of the team who worked on them. In his obituary in *The Stage*, it says that he became the lynchpin of forces broadcasting in Delhi before going on to produce the *Calling Blighty* films, which was 'entirely his idea' (*The Stage* 1988: 8). He certainly played a vital role in the filming. In February 1945, it was reported that the filming of *Calling Blighty* and arrangements for recording messages from troops in India 'are organised by Captain Stephen McCormack in conjunction with the Directors of Services Kinematography, All India Radio, BBC and enthusiastic welfare officers in India and South East Asia Command'. At that point, 11,250 greetings were handled annually, but this must have included radio greetings as well as the filmed messages. It was the ambition at that point to increase the number by four times over the coming year 1945 (All Forces 1945).

However, McCormack was only posted to Army Broadcasting at GHQ in January 1944, five months after the first screenings of the films in Britain. His diary from 20 December 1943 records that he arrived in Bangalore to 'find Jack Frost still wants me for *Calling Blighty* with Captaincy. But what do ENSA want?' (McCormack 1943: n.pag.). Major Jack Frost, the former 'Uncle Jack' of the BBC, who would read his wireless yarns on Children's Hour radio in the 1920s, is ultimately credited as the inventor of the idea. 'So enthusiastic was the reception when the idea was first tried out that the War office cabled its congratulations to Major Jack Frost who originated the feature and is now responsible for its development in India [...]. When we have increased our staff we shall take film units up to the forward areas and film the hometown boys against their local background said Major Frost [...] Ultimately there will not be a single place in Britain that will be unrepresented' (Ballymena Observer 1944: 3).

Frost had been the originator of the *Your Family Album* (1942) programme, which consisted of a series of interviews with relatives by a War Office representative who called on them and described the everyday incidents of life in their homes. The interview was flown to India and broadcast to the troops by Frost himself. He is cited as the officer who 'Suggested and developed the *Calling Blighty* greetings film series' although he returned to England when the scheme was up and running in June 1944 because of the illness of his daughter. He had been assistant to the BBC chief engineer in the Savoy Hill days, and went to India to work on military wireless installations, before taking up welfare work. 'While in hospital the idea of special broadcast greetings facilities for the troops occurred to him; he planned the scheme as he lay in bed, and when he was discharged he was ordered to put his proposals into effect' (*Middlesex Chronicle* 1944: 6). Who ordered him to do this is unclear. An article in *The Stage* suggests it might have been Major Brian Cave-Brown Cave, about whom 'we recall your entertainment interest as the instigator of *Calling Blighty* and other worthy aspirations that revived tired fighting forces overseas' (*The Stage* 1953). Frost also suggested a parallel *Calling India* scheme where relatives in the United Kingdom would make films that would be screened to men in the Far East. A small number of these was made in early 1945, possibly twelve, under the title *A Letter from Home* by a film crew from the Army Kinematograph Service based at Wembley, but none appears to have survived (Sargent 1992: 2).

The production facilities for the *Blighty* films already existed in Bombay through the Training Film Centre, later to become the Combined Kinematograph Services Film Production and Training Centre, abbreviated to the CKS (Sargent 1992: 3). This existed to make training films for the Indian Army; the production offices were based at Caltex House, acquired from the Esso oil company, and the studio space was rented from the Shree Sound Studios. Adam Becket, who worked on the production side recalled 'The CKS was purely in Bombay to make educational films for the Indian Army. It seemed a logical thing when they wanted these "living letters" to toss it to us to do that for them' (Becket 1992). The centre, as Paul Sargent points out, had the infrastructure and film technicians, both Indian and British, the labs for processing of the film existed in Bombay, as well as the production offices, and all it needed was the spark of the idea, and the almost 400 films of the *Calling Blighty* series were brought into being.

A film editor at Caltex house was solely employed in working on the films after they had been processed and printed. The musical title sequences and end credit, which were pre-produced had to be added, and the soundtrack synced with the picture and cuts made to exclude extraneous material. These were usually minimal, and some films apart from the credits were virtually a single uninterrupted shot; however, some directors had made more creative versions that required more sophisticated editing. The sound was mixed so that it was balanced, and a safety print taken in case of loss in transit and then the resulting film negative was sent by sea to the United Kingdom, a journey that took around six weeks in all. They were dispatched to the Denham studios in Uxbridge where a distribution print was made and the films sent onwards to the regional cinemas for screening (Sargent 1992: 4). The resources required to make the films in wartime were vast. The soldiers had to be flown to Bombay grouped by city or region or trucks filled with heavy equipment and crew driven on immense journeys into war-torn Burma. The films needed a monthly quota of scarce raw film stock, which was committed by the War Office after the success of the first test screenings and editing and printing. There was then a similar organisational effort back in the United Kingdom to arrange for all the families to be grouped together and screenings integrated into cinema schedules.

It is an immense achievement that nearly 400 were produced and presented, films made 5000 miles away often in wartime conditions. But the significance of the films is not only in their content but their uniqueness, both in the way the voice of the ordinary serviceman is captured and preserved, but in their status. They are the first films of their kind in the world, and what was originated for utilitarian purposes has become freighted with meaning, the first mass unscripted filmed voices.

4

I'm in the Pink:
An Overview of the Messages

It was a Heath Robinson Pinewood. The exterior was corrugated iron – you can imagine the sound of the rain on that. The sound-proofing was cowpats sprayed onto the walls.

(Len Abbott, sound recordist, on the Shree Studios Bombay [Abbott 1991: n.pag.])

Albert Becket who worked on the studio-based *Calling Blighty* productions called them 'talking letters', and indeed they were essentially filmed letters home or in their brevity, often more like talking postcards. But despite this, they reveal much more about the men, their circumstances, their state of mind and the subtext of the war they were engaged in, than the simple format ostensibly offered. There was a typical pattern of message, where a man would greet his hometown and relatives, say that he was doing fine, getting his mail regularly (or not), and then say goodbye and handover to the next man. Hence Lawrence Yarwood's introduction by the previous soldier and message to his family in Sheffield: 'Now Mrs Yarwood here's a surprise for you'. 'Hello Joan darling, how are you keeping? Well I hope. And you Winsome' (his five-year-old daughter, who also came to the screening 73 years later), 'you were quite a little girl when I left you. Possibly not recognise your Pop; still I hope you're keeping well. Hello Mum and Dad, and Jean. Mail is coming through quite well; I'd like a lot more though. Well cheerio for now' (*CB* 86 1944).

Of the 391 issues known to have been filmed, 60 have survived, which is remarkable in itself, but they are concentrated for unknown reasons in certain parts of the country. Thus 23 are of the Manchester area alone, a legacy of a fortunate find of the rusting film cans in the basement of the Manchester Town Hall, when the building was being refurbished in the 1980s. Instead of being discarded, they were passed on to the North West Film Archive for preservation, and the present Director Marion Hewitt drew the author's attention to this rich find when

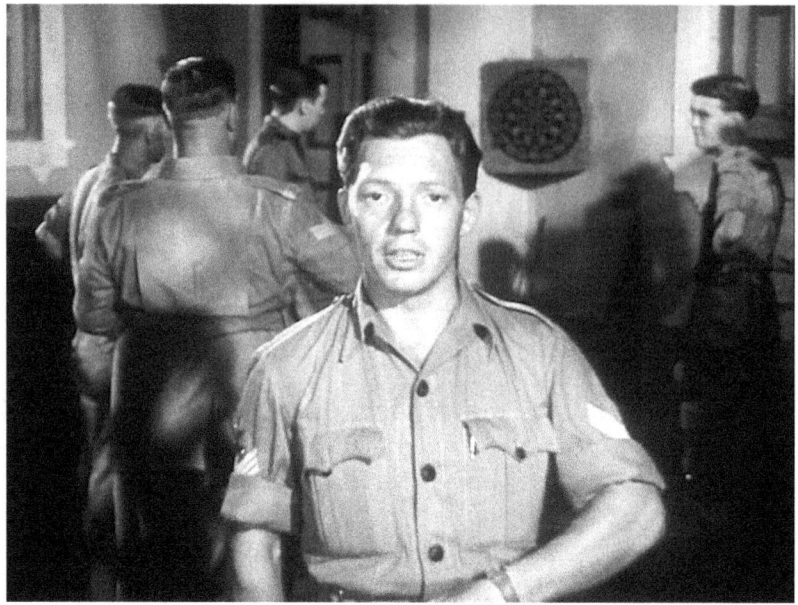

FIGURE 4.1: Lawrence Yarwood in the Bombay studio (*CB* 86 1944). © BFI.

the author discussed the films with her, and they decided together to launch a project to trace the relatives.

Seven films are known that feature men from Sheffield and South Yorkshire, five from Brighton, four from Dundee and the rest are single issues or at most two from scattered towns and cities around the country – Glasgow, Northampton, Norwich, Leicester and several other places, mostly in the north of England. There are large gaps in coverage of the United Kingdom; no issues are known to exist from Northern Ireland or London, the West Country or Wales, for example. However, in the regionality of the films, from many parts of Britain, they create a picture of men, their accents and speech, regional references and songs, which bring to life a film portrait of the United Kingdom at a time when such a thing did not exist.

Lawrence Yarwood was speaking from what appeared to be a NAAFI canteen in India, with men sitting at tables drinking tea or beer, often wreathed in clouds of smoke, and attended by Indian servants, and others playing cards or darts. In fact the canteen was an elaborate film set at the Shree sound studios in Bombay, where men were gathered together from widely distant parts of India or Burma, sometimes from different regiments but always from the same city or area (Sargent 1992: 29).

But there was another kind of film, shot on location using mobile newsreel trucks with portable filming equipment, which followed the men to camps and locations in the theatre of war. The location films presented opportunities for creative

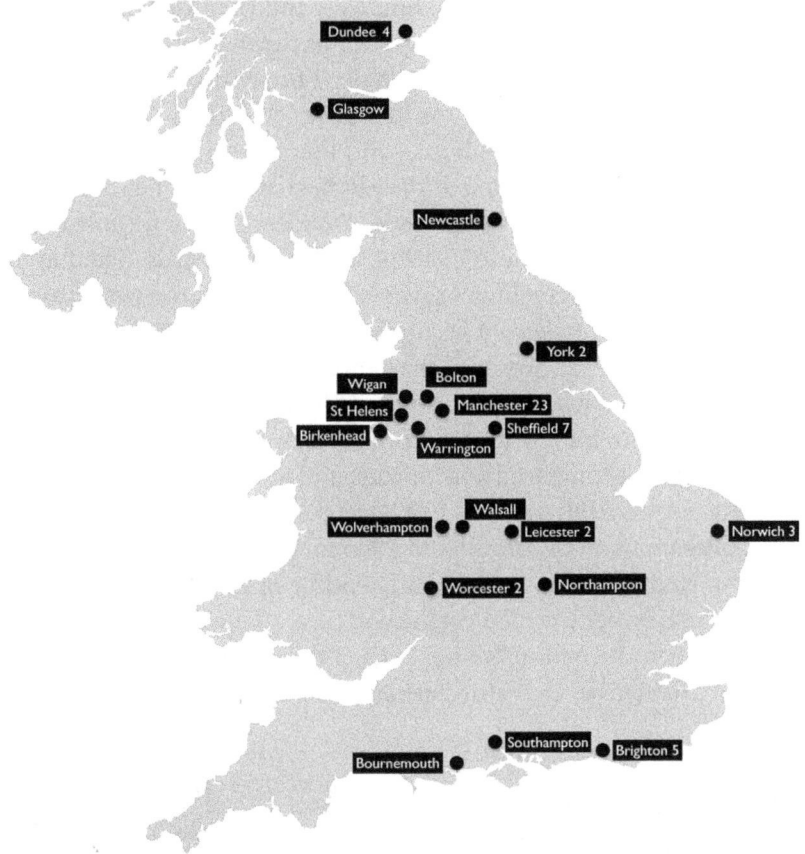

FIGURE 4.2: Distribution of surviving *Calling Blighty* films across the United Kingdom. © Steve Hawley.

treatment by the largely unknown directors of the films, and there are many examples of rather forced dramatic scenarios that act as a prologue to the men who then turn to the audience to deliver their messages. These quasi-fictional introductions sit awkwardly as framing devices within the direct Skype-like address.

The studio-based films came first and were augmented by location filming from mid-1944 onwards, although the first film that still exists is a studio issue, number 35 from Dundee. This is fairly typical of the studio-based reels; it opens with a title sequence of the Gateway to India arch in Bombay, and then in a single shot, men walk up to the camera to deliver their messages. There is music in the background, apparently orchestral music from records, and the men all sing a regional song at the end accompanied by a piano in the studio, in this case Loch Lomond, but this particular film is unusual in that the men also sing a traditional folk song at the beginning – Bonnie Dundee – and then deliver their wishes to family members and talk about the regularity of the mail and desire to be home. More than one mentions the local dance hall: 'I hope to get that dance with you at the Locarno', or thanks a friend for items sent to India – 'Jean who has been very kind in sending me all of my books and literature and so forth'. One sends best wishes to his workmates 'back at the old firm at Valentines', referring to the famous photographic company Valentines of Dundee, known for its topographical views of Scotland, which was sold in 1994 to Hallmark cards. The film is a little shorter than the usual *Blighty* film at seven and a half minutes; they usually ran to 10 or 12 minutes, but in essence it is similar to the pattern of greetings films that continued with some variations until they ended in 1946 (*CB 35 1944*).

Recorded interviews with production staff held at the Imperial War Museum show that the servicemen's self-presentation, which sometimes looks rehearsed in the similarity of the greetings and awkwardness of address, was not determined by the filmmakers or ostensibly censored. When asked about scripting, Jack Atcheler who was a cameraman on the films from 1945 and then spent a lifetime in the film industry (he started as a focus puller on David Lean's *In Which We Serve* 1942) said he did not remember the men ever doing that. 'We would ask the guy next to (the speaker) to introduce him. We never gave them any ... they could just go on chatting. I don't remember ever stopping anyone talking' (Atcheler 1991: n.pag.).

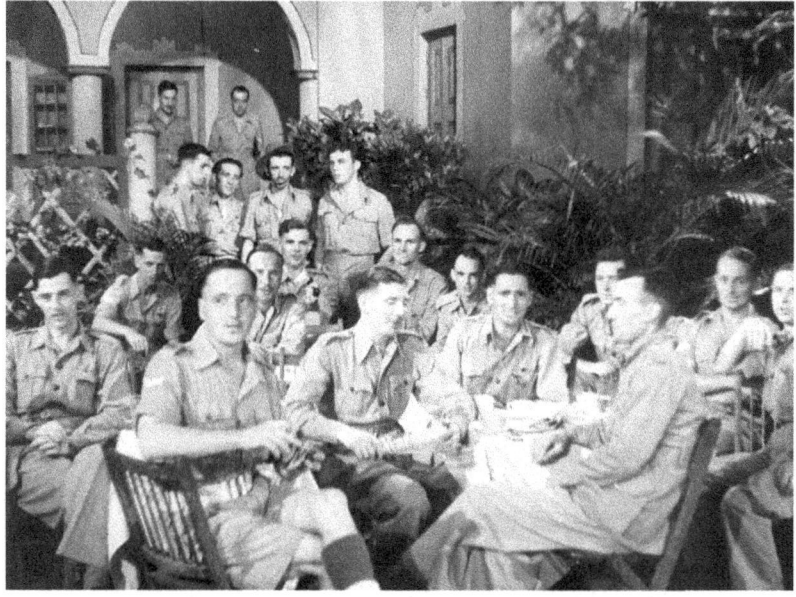

FIGURE 4.3: Soldiers in the Shree Sound Studios film set. © IWM.

Len Abbott who was a sound recordist concurs. 'There wasn't any rehearsal factor, they were schooled a little as to what it was for, other than that it was spontane- ous. I don't believe there was any time limit, there was a lot of embarrassment there' (Abbott 1992: n.pag.).

Although the basic pattern of the films in the studio and on location was the same, the men came to the camera or the camera came to them as they delivered their messages, there were differences between the two operations. The studio had a fixed film set, the 'NAAFI canteen', although it was an idealized version of the real thing, a full crew and the lighting and production resources of a complete studio. It took normally two days to produce an issue, and they aimed for ten issues a month (Becket 1992: n.pag.). There was a chance for a rehearsal with the camera, as the set enabled a slightly more sophisticated camera treatment, with camera tracks and other film techniques, and the men could rehearse slightly their parts and be corrected if necessary. The Shree Studios also had extensive grounds outside, and often the directors would take men into their surroundings to film them against palm trees or more exotic foliage. They used the Mitchell 35mm camera, also employed in professional Hollywood films at the time, and 'all the usual cumbersome sound equipment of those days'. The men were flown in and then brought in on lorries, all from a particular city or region, many of them fresh from battle against the Japanese. 'Some of them were a bit hard, they had been up through Burma, they had a bad time, they really didn't care too much about discipline' (Abbott 1992: n.pag.). One of those was Tag Barnes, who, however, contrary to this comes over as a rather matter-of-fact and at ease with his situa- tion. Whilst most of the remaining films were made in India and Burma, at least one was filmed in Ceylon, present-day Sri Lanka and one or more in Malaya, at the historic Penang racecourse.

The film was edited in the Bombay labs and then the negative was flown to London, and in the studio films at least, it was shot in such a way that if a man was killed in action, his contribution could be edited out. However, this did not always happen, nor was it sometimes possible. In one of the rare *Calling Blighty* films from Ceylon, 'Here among the wonderful ruins of Polonnaruwa' as it starts, 'some boys from Dundee' were filmed in 1945 at an airbase, among them a Flight Lt Bennett, pictured speaking over some bushes: 'I'm feeling alright and fairly fit. Ceylon's not too bad a place' (*CB* 186 1945). In January 1945, the parents of Flight-Lieutenant J. Wallace Bennett went to see a film of him at The King's Theatre Dundee, despite the fact that he had been reported missing in action in the Far East. The film had been shot before he took off on his last flight, and in fact as welfare officer for his station in Ceylon, he had been largely responsible for the making of this particular film. It can be imagined the mixture of emotions felt by his family in the audience, as from the screen he greeted his parents and sister 'I hope Mum and Dad managed through. If Mum is there, my fondest love to you and Shena and Dad'. His father said at the time: 'This afternoon has been a joy to us to see and hear him once more. We are not giving up hope yet' (*Daily Record* 1945: n.pag.).

The films made on location did not lend themselves to elaborate staging: 'We found a decent location, a few pagodas; nice background' (Atcheler 1991: n.pag.). Then the men were spread around in groups of twos and threes or just arranged in a group from where one after another would run up to a prearranged mark, deliver their message and run back. In the location film unit, there were usually three sound technicians, the cameraman and his assistant and the director. In addition, there was a welfare officer who would go on in advance to the regiments and organize the filming (Atcheler 1991: n.pag.).

Dick Fiddament from the Royal Norfolk Regiment described some decades later for the Imperial War Museum, the experience of being filmed by the *Calling Blighty* crew just outside Mandalay that had just been taken by the 14th Army. He explains that the shoot had been organized by the Director of Welfare and Amenities. 'Sam Hornor was on it (the company commander). It was a respite. We were at a place, the river in the background is the Irrawaddy. I can't say they picked the elite, there were a lot of my company in there, the message came round that we could be on film and it would be shown at the Haymarket in Norwich,

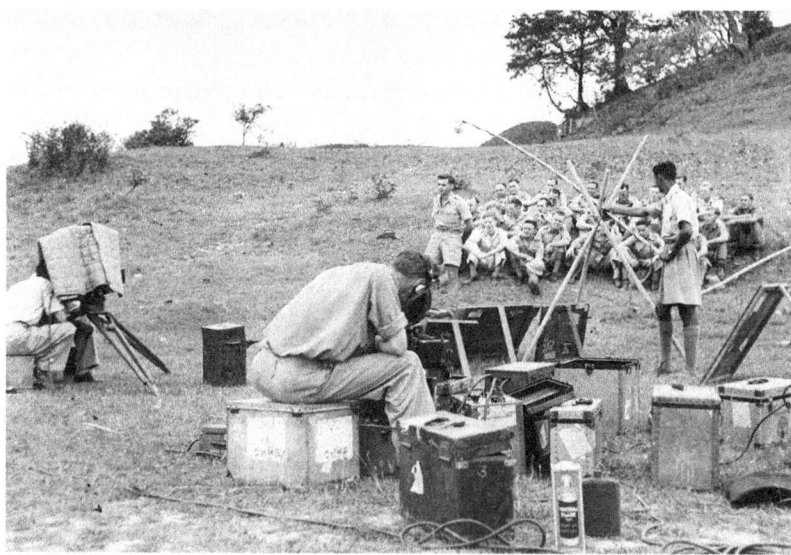

FIGURE 4.4: A *Calling Blighty* film crew prepares to film Royal Air Force personnel from Sheffield in a forward area on the Burma Front. © IWM.

and our parents, they could take their friends and see this, and also the film that was being currently showing' (Fiddament 1997: n.pag.). He regarded the film as a little bit of propaganda as evidenced by Captain Hornor's comment about having the Japanese on the run, although such an overt reference to triumph and the war was in fact rare. The production team set the cameras up and put up sheets of metal as reflectors instead of lights, which focussed the burning sun even though it was already very hot. 'What you did was, there were a couple or three of you come down together. When my turn came, Jackie Brown, he was a pal of mine, he says hello Hilda, which was his wife, hello darling and all the rest of the mushy stuff. I'm at an end; he says here's my old pal which was me and you say your piece. Hello Mum and Dad because I was single, and my sister and brother-in-law. Well you do [work out what to say beforehand] or you'll forget it, first time ever. it sounds easy and I'll tell you now, my brother who was in the Marines when he heard it, he said what a prat, you look a right tool'. He notes that there were men from the Batallion who were filmed on that occasion who were later killed because there was still action (Fiddament 1997: n.pag.). Sam Hornor himself was more critical of his own performance. 'We were interviewed by the BBC chap [sic] and said all the right things and sent messages. That was shown at the Haymarket cinema [Norwich]. I heard the thing afterwards; I've never heard anybody sound so pompous and dreadful. I said, we've got the Jap on the run, terrible pompous remark. But they all enjoyed it' (Hornor 1997: n.pag.).

Synchronized sound on film was still a relatively new innovation in location filming, having been invented in the United States in the late 1920s, and Charles Lindbergh was recorded briefly for a newsreel in 1927 at the take-off of his record-breaking cross Atlantic flight. Mussolini was filmed the same year making a speech in his self-described 'very imperfect English', albeit highly scripted, and George Bernard Shaw made what may have been the first impromptu talk in his garden for Fox Movietone in 1930. Apparently directed by himself, Shaw pretended to be surprised by the camera, rambled at length and impersonated satirically Mussolini's earlier performance on screen, but this may have been the first improvised and informal performance captured in sound and vision. However, American newsreels did not on the whole enthusiastically develop the possibilities for informal interviews available to the medium and continued the use of what was in essence novelty celebrity footage (Fielding 2011: n.pag.). The equipment was also heavy and had to be transported in a specially adapted truck. Other interviews were conducted in newsreels, and a rare audience with Mahatma Ghandi was filmed in 1931. There was even a commercial anti-war film about World War I, *Forgotten Men* made in 1934 that had a series of 'interviews' with ex-servicemen conducted by military historian Sir John Hammerton. The men appear very deferential before their questioner, who elicits very slow and stiff answers to his leading questions, and their answers take up about six minutes of the feature-length film, so this was not a precursor to an informal documentary style, but it did at least include a range of nationalities including a Belgian, Italian and even two German ex-combatant's voices (Norman Lee 1934: n.pag.).

The camera employed for the *Calling Blighty* films on location was an Akeley, with 1000 foot magazines of 35mm film. The Akeley was a well-known US newsreel and documentary camera – it had been developed as a field camera in the 1920s and was used by many naturalists. In particular, it was employed in silent mode by Robert Flaherty in 1922 for *Nanook of the North*, the documentary classic considered the first real ethnographic film, about the life of an Inuit hunter. To start with the sound was recorded on a separate 'camera', which required a separate 35mm film reel onto which the audio was recorded optically; Len Abbott the sound recordist recalls it as being RCA equipment, an RCA N23 or R23 recorder (Abbott 1992: n.pag.). This required vastly increased resources as well as twice the amount of film, a further support truck, batteries and extra sound equipment. But on the second tour, this had been replaced by recording the sound directly onto the same film that recorded the picture, as a box four inches high attached to the camera recorded the audio on the side of the film strip, which meant a much lighter equipment load. The crew still needed a portable mixer, sound boom, microphone and reflectors for use instead of heavy lights, in addition to the 100,000 or 200,000 feet of highly flammable 35mm PlusX black-and-white negative film, but the total load could be fitted into a 30 hundredweight Ford or Chevrolet six-wheel drive truck with another smaller truck for bedding and camping equipment. The team would stop in major towns where they could in Burma or Malaya, such as Mandalay, or sometimes smaller towns, travelling overland, often slowly through roads potholed from mines. They would stay in requisitioned houses organized by the welfare officer, having no headquarters to go back to, and eat with the regiments they were filming; otherwise they were living on K rations. They avoided overt fighting; however, the Japanese were being pushed back through Burma at that time, and there were still snipers about and warning signs at the entrance to villages 'Do not stop or slow down in this village'. Abbott's films were directed by their larger-than-life Australian director, Lorraine Hamilton-Webb, often seen smoking a big cigar: 'As soon as he arrived he said call me Ham. He was a typical Australian, bit brash and extrovert. He could chivvy them along and they loved him' (Abbott 1992: n.pag.).

The men in the films were volunteers, who seemed enthusiastic about the opportunity to send their filmed message home. 'Did it change morale? They came down there highly elated, that someone was looking after their welfare at last [...] they weren't looked after, they were forgotten' (Atcheler 1991: n.pag.). As in Lawrence Yarwood's case, the message is often straightforward, a postcard-like greeting to named members of the family, comments on the frequency of the mail or lack of it, a self-description, 'As you can see I'm in the pink', and a general exhortation to keep your chins up and keep smiling. The messages were not an informal interview of the kind we are used to today, and in any case that approach to speaking on screen was unknown at the time, but rather self-authored statements, where the fact of being seen on screen at all speaking in one's own voice was more important in many cases than what was being said. But besides the standard formula, that seems not imposed, but rather fallen into naturally by men filmed in very different places at different times, there were other modes of expression that shine a light on the position of men in the 14th Army, very far from Britain, some of whom had been away on active service without leave for many years.

So some men were able to transcend the artificial situation and speak with subdued emotion straight from the heart: 'However I look, I'm still the same in heart and mind and longings, and full of appreciation for your own affection. Lift up your heart bright eyes, be in God's keeping' (*CB* 52 1944). 'I was particularly thinking of you on the tenth of August. We shall soon have the realisation of our dreams and be together again. And, God willing, we will spend our next anniversary together' (*CB* 85 1944). This openness of masculine expression in screen-based communication may be more common now, but it was completely unknown at the time except in letters, and given the very public

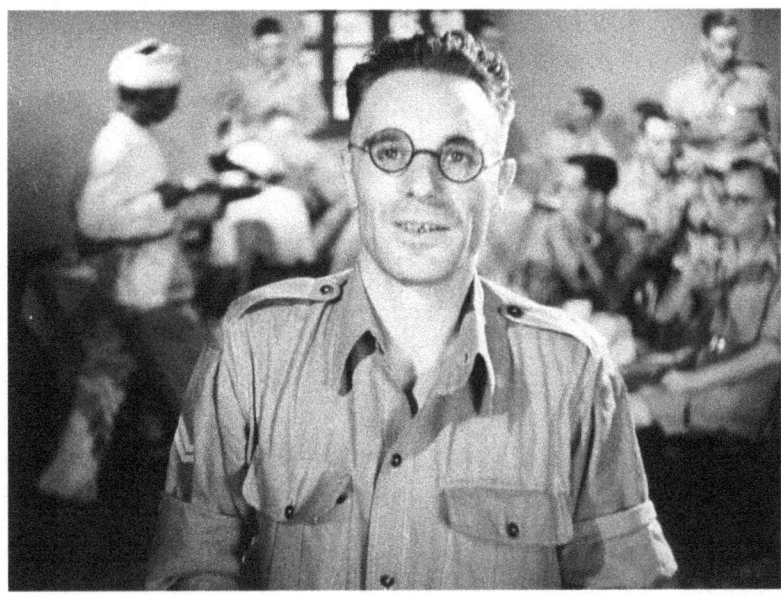

FIGURE 4.5: Cecil Rhodes. 'I love you. Lift up your heart, bright eyes' (*CB* 52 1944). © IWM.

nature of both the filming and the anticipated cinema projection, required a subtle understanding of the impact of the personal message on the family in the audience. Not many of the men could achieve this, but it is not surprising, it would have required a screen actor's understanding of the emotional impact of the close-up, the direct address to camera, and there were precious few of those in the Fourteenth Army.

Many men also spoke of or to their children, sometimes dimly remembered, and in some cases who had only been born after they had travelled overseas, often with a similar degree of tenderness. 'Hello Marie, hello Michael. Just want you to know darling you're always in my thoughts, and I only long for the day when I'll come back to you and our Michael. God bless you both' (*CB* 191 1945). 'Well Gillian, here's your Daddy that you don't know, but who's looking to the day when he can see you and tell you how much he loves you' (*CB* 210 1945). 'I hope that Sheila is not disappointed to see her Daddy for the first time' (*CB* 86 1944). Events in Britain had moved on in the long period since the men had left home, as we see with Louis Schimberg, and men had been overseas for up to six years. Close family members may have died, and it was difficult to find a public form of address to mark such deep feelings, thousands of miles away in the Burmese jungle. 'It was only a couple of days ago that I heard of Mother's sad passing. By the time that you see this film, much of that acute sorrow will be supplanted by the happy memories we have of Mother' (*CB* 273 1946). Seemingly impromptu, Corporal Hickling manages to find a form of words that not only expresses the nature of the loss but also provides some positivity that the *Blighty* messages encouraged. It was a difficult feat to pull off.

There were references to family members in other theatres of war – 'I'm glad to hear our Eddie got home from Africa all right. That's one of us anyway' (*CB* 311 1946) – but mostly any reference at all to the war is surprisingly absent. Men smoke incessantly, both on the screen delivering messages and in the background, and express their thanks for cigarettes sent to them, 'which I'm smoking'. One man delivers his whole message, 'As regards repat [repatriation back to Blighty] you can confidently expect me home by August', without taking his pipe from his mouth (*CB* 212 1945). There are frequent references to food and drink; one Norwich man wistfully yearns for a pint of his local beer, and another from Leicester teasingly says he has brought his family a bunch of bananas and holds up the bunch to prove it. At the time in ration book in Britain, such exotic fruits were unobtainable, and the glimpse of seeming tropical luxury served to emphasize the apparent wellbeing of the men in the Far East. Some men were filmed frolicking in the sea at Malabar Bay in Bombay: 'Hello this is from India' (*CB* 380 1946). Other scenes were filmed on the beach, as a group of men with a performing monkey accompanying a small local child address the camera or another group walk along the beach followed silently by an Indian lifeguard. The sun beat down, and even in black and white, the impression aimed at war-torn Britain was something of an exotic foreign holiday, the war very far away. However, the fact that this was an illusion was pointedly referred to by one or two of the men; 'These surroundings, they look very good, but I'd rather be at Heaton Park any day' (*CB* 203 1945).

There were frequent local references, emphasizing the films' status as a small Domesday book of film in wartime, crystallizing in each film a specific accent and song and regional identity from all parts of the United Kingdom. 'I'll hope you'll be down at the Willows, or are you supporting the Reds again?', one man from Manchester says about his local rugby team (*CB* 361 1946). A Brighton man longs for 'first of all a sight of you, and then a sight of the Sussex downs' (*CB* 151 1945). Wilf Parker from Wadsley Bridge in Sheffield, obviously a Sheffield Wednesday supporter, remembers the Wadsley bridge club where he used to have a pint as well as Jackie Robinson, the Sheffield and England player who infamously was forced with his team to give the Nazi salute when playing an international in Germany in 1938 (*CB* 252 1946). Another man, Jim from Bolton, spends much more of his message reminiscing about his favourite pastime and local places than greeting his relatives: 'I received the parcel of Cycling, (a magazine) from cousin Bert the other day and I was very pleased to see some sketches by Frank Patterson, you know, Piccadilly farm, Belmont, Withnall, the Wilson

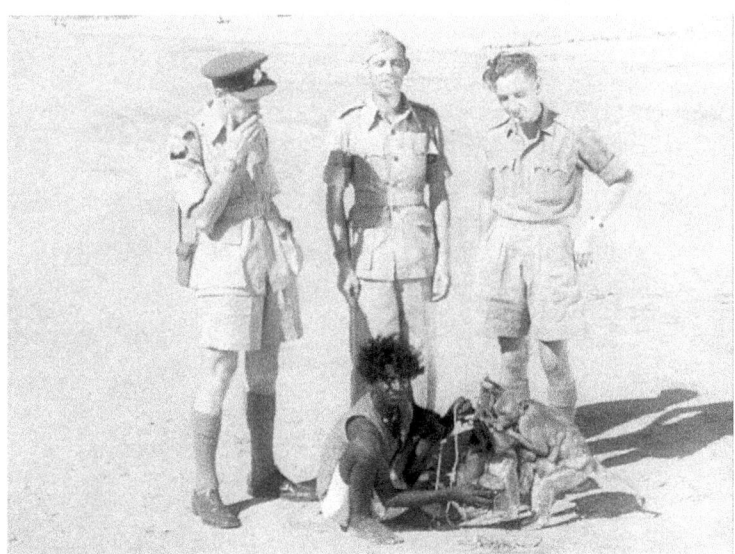

FIGURE 4.6: Sheffield men on Malabar beach Bombay. © BFI.

arms. Oh it was good to see those places again. All I'm waiting for is the time when I'm in the saddle again. Just to see them in reality. Oh it's great, it is really. Well Mum I'm afraid I can't speak too very long, you see I have an appointment with Dorothy Lamour' (he coquettishly holds up his hand to his chin and then as Harry Allen plays the closing music on piano performs an extravagant sand dance) (*CB* 1945).

Mindful of the very public nature of the reception of the films, few men were prepared to risk a more intimate message, but a small number hinted at it. 'She'll probably be worried I don't write enough. Well actually what I wanted to write wouldn't be passed by the censor' (*CB* 82 1944). 'Hello David this is your father. If you're a good boy I'll see what I can do to get a little sister for you. Now you've got Mummy blushing' (*CB* 86 1944). And one Manchester man speaking from somewhere in Burma neatly encapsulates his desire for home comforts: 'I miss some fish and chips and a pint now and again you know. But I'll soon be home and then we'll get up them stairs' (*CB* 203 1945). (His comrades laugh and one gives the thumbs up sign and says '*Thik Hai*' meaning okay in army Indian slang.)

There are a few references to the war, most of them upbeat: 'All of us boys here are going to win the war' (*CB* 151 1944). But the reality of combat and the dangers they faced are noticeably absent apart from in a handful of films. The one remembered by Dick Fiddament from 1945 opens with a pan across the Irrawaddy

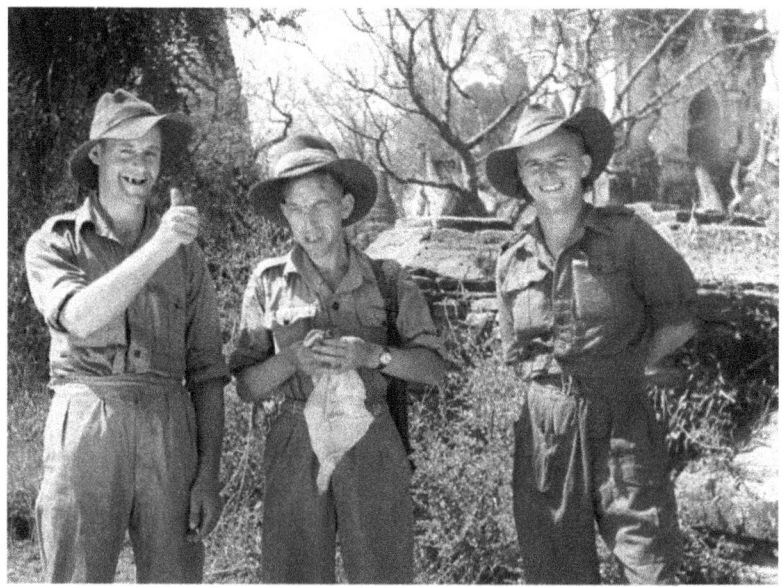

FIGURE 4.7: 'Thik Hai' from Burma (*CB* 203 1945). © IWM.

River and the Ava railway bridge spanning the river, which had been destroyed by the 14th Army to prevent the Japanese retreating across it, and continues in the ruins of the streets of Mandalay. Captain Hornor of the Royal Norfolk Regiment, the same Captain Horner who later described his filming experience for the Imperial War Museum, in a rather upper-class drawl, delivers the only message in the films that still exist, that focuses solely on the war, emphasizing the symbolic nature of the fall of Mandalay in the retaking of Burma. He is also the only man who does not personally greet a relative. 'As you probably know, the regiment has been honoured with the privilege of marching through the city with full honours, and we're very proud of that. We've really got the Japs on the run this time, and we're going to keep on at them until we run them right out of Burma ... Remember we've not forgotten Singapore, and first at Kohima and now in Burma we are having our revenge' (*CB* 206 1945). In a few words, he flags up the trajectory of defeat and then much later retaliation at the turning point in the battle of Kohima/Imphal, in the gradual emergence of a hard-won triumph. Other men in the same film echo this sentiment: 'I am looking forward to the joys of victory'. 'We will soon have this job finished'.

In the *Calling Blighty* film numbered 205, shot just before the Norfolk film, the aftermath of the battle for Mandalay is clearly visible and mentioned by the men from Worcester and Kidderminster. 'This is Mandalay, well what's left of it'. The men all hold rifles or machine guns, a rare public exhibition in the films of the tools of war, and the tone is determined whilst acknowledging the bitterness of the battle. 'Really tough time, well still, never matter'. 'What you think of this as a souvenir? This is one that will not get back to Japan', as the man holds out a flag featuring the emblem of the rising sun. Sergeant Major White DSM walks towards the camera with a half-smoked cigar in his mouth carrying his rifle, with the background of Mandalay in ruins: 'The going's been tough, but we've seen the job through. Looking at me, we of the Fourteenth Army *will* see the job through'. There are also rare hints of casualties: 'Corporal Greenhough of the stretcher bearers. He's one of those fellows that catch us up'. Mandalay had been taken in March 1945, and the battle had been fierce, but even through the fatigue of victory, there was a half-hearted attempt to reference the picturesque East. 'Here I am in the middle of the ruins of Mandalay. Not a very pretty scene at present, but it's quite alright I suppose, in peacetime' (*CB* 205 1945).

The *Calling Blighty* films in their technique were simple although made with great professionalism and attention to detail, both in terms of cinematography and sound recording. They were nearly all second-person testimony in the sense of addressed to the viewer, spoken directly to camera, the subject looking straight at us, which is one of the aspects that give them the power they still retain today. There were hardly any occasions on which an interviewer was present in the shot although rarely a senior officer would appear in the frame, emphasizing the differences in rank and status in the forces and somewhat uneasily dominating the scene, and overshadowing the deliverer of the message. The class and authority divisions of leadership in the forces, as in fiction films of the period, are barely concealed.

The films made on location in Burma or Malaya tended to be uncomplicated, a group of men sitting in front of a hill where one after another would run up to the camera, or groups of twos or threes standing in front of a bit of local colour like a pagoda, where they handed over from one to the next. But the studio-based films, especially those that were filmed in the grounds of the sound studio or on the nearby beach, sometimes had a senior officer who would introduce the concept of the film. 'You chaps all come from Manchester? Well that's fine. Welcome to *Calling Blighty*. Now if you'll just make yourselves comfortable and disperse yourselves around these grounds here, we'll bring the camera around to you'. The same officer stays in shot as the first two men deliver their messages, and after the first one spoken says 'There you are you see, it's very easy isn't it?'. The effect somewhat inhibits the spontaneity of the men, but of course whether or not the senior welfare officer or other senior staff actually appear, they would've been there behind the camera, and this perhaps accounts for the stilted nature of a lot of the messages. 'Now you're not nervous are you?'. 'No sir'. 'Good. Who are you going to talk to? Well there she is in front' (*CB* 241 1946).

In most of the films, the formula is relatively simple, a message to camera, and a handover and brief introduction to the next man (or woman). But in the films made at the Shree Sound Studios and around the exteriors in Bombay, in the studio grounds or on the beach at Malabar Bay, there are interesting sequences where the unknown directors use the language of film to mask the disjuncture between an objective (third-person) camera shot and a second-person piece to camera. These sequences strike us still as awkward but also hint at another kind of film, a more documentary approach, perhaps derived from the training films that the CKS had been making in Bombay. They also act as a window, in a very subdued way, and allow us to look in on some aspects of the everyday lives of the servicemen although there are obviously no overt depictions of active service against the Japanese, with the rare exceptions mentioned. There were limits to what could be portrayed to a home audience of wives and families who were ignorant of the true horrors of the Far East war.

So, in one film, a lorry is stuck in the sand at Malabar Bay, as a group of men, all from Sheffield, try to free it. A disembodied voice, not an objective voiceover but the authoritarian voice of the Army, ask them what they are doing, and one man responds that he is 'trying to find this film unit, this *Calling Blighty* business'. The army voice tells them 'This is it anyway, you can carry on from where

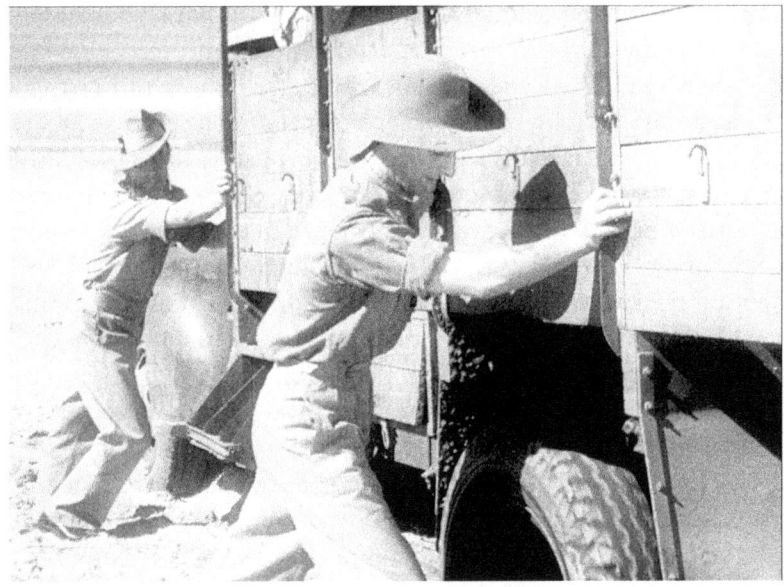

FIGURE 4.8: A lorry manned by Sheffield men 'stuck' on Malabar Beach (*CB* 380 1946). © BFI.

you are'. The soldier answers 'Oh I'm glad it is. This is it Wilkie', whereupon the men address the camera one by one to send messages to the Sheffield families (*CB* 380 1946). The situation is obviously concocted; why were the men be driving on the beach to find 'this *Calling Blighty* business'? And why would they not be aware of the camera in front of them. In an era where almost everyone possesses a pocket video camera, and a relationship between the device and the images being recorded is obvious, these sequences where the apparatus of film-making is unacknowledged and invisible seem anachronistic. This is especially so as we know now the paraphernalia of recording would have been extensive; a large 35mm camera, sound recording on a separate camera, the crew members, the lights or reflectors, all of which would have been highly noticeable in the 1940s. But few being filmed at the time or in the audience would have seen a film camera in that era, and the sequences would have been read very differently by the home cinema audiences in 1944.

There are several sequences portrayed, which are variations on the theme of a man writing a letter home with pen and paper, who is told off-screen or by another soldier beside him 'Why not speak to your family directly?'. So that in the Bombay studio set, a leisurely pan over a man walking through the mocked up-canteen brings him to two others sitting at a table apparently writing. In a long and stilted sequence filmed in the third person, the men make conversation. 'Say haven't we met somewhere before Sergeant?' 'Yes I think so.' 'What's your name?' 'Chris Hayward. Sit down will you. What part of Manchester do you come from?' 'Old Trafford, Manchester'. The scene continues as he reveals he is writing to his mother and father, and then the film cuts to a second-person close-up as he delivers his message directly instead (*CB* 328 1946). The purpose of these establishing shots seems to be to show the ease of speaking directly, which was then a radical and previously almost unknown innovation, rather than the time-consuming production of a written message, but as the filmed introduction uses film stock that could have shown another possible two messages, perhaps these low-key dramatic interludes added a certain filmic interest for their makers to the rather pedestrian (for the directors) message to camera.

The films being '"See me hear me" film snaps' are mostly examples of second-person narration or direct address to the camera. This is an uncommon point of view for film, which is mostly shot from the perspective of an objective third person, although very rarely the first person is used where we 'see' through the eyes of the camera. The second-person perspective was common in the early years of cinema and of course is ubiquitous today on laptops and handheld mobile devices through video calls, Facetime and Zoom conferencing, but it was very rare in the cinema at the time the films were made and remains rare in contemporary film as a fictional device. This adds to the shock and intimacy of our reception of the films in the cinema even now, despite the individuals being unknown to us, as we are unused to direct address on a large screen. Nor is second-person address in literature, a novel addressed to 'you', a very common literary device, being employed mostly for instructional or self-help books. Even by 1910, cinema had changed so that the protagonist looking directly at the camera was regarded as breaking our voyeuristic looking in on a fictional world. 'The sense of reality is destroyed and the hypnotic illusion that has taken possession of the spectator's mind, holding him by the power of visual suggestion, is gone' (Brown 2012: 5).

In cinema films, the look to camera is usually fleeting and intended to create a humorous bond with the audience (Groucho Marx or Woody Allen), or perhaps a contemplative moment of stillness. One of the few instances in mainstream cinema is in *Singing in the Rain* (1952), wherein a demonstration film within the film, a 'novelty' is shown at a party that demonstrates the then-new technology of synchronized speaking with picture, a graduation from silent film ridiculed by the film industry partygoers. This direct address film, supposedly by the inventor of this new process, has some similarities with the *Calling Blighty* films; it is remarkably immediate and a shock within the conventional narrative of the musical film we are watching. It is also (and unlike the *Blighty* films) due to the exaggerated performance of the supposed inventor, also slightly creepy; no wonder the audience felt that it would never catch on. The theatrical tradition this confounds is termed 'breaking the fourth wall' where the illusion that we are in the theatre gazing on actors who cannot see us is dissolved. Seeing the *Calling Blighty* films on a handheld device the effect is minimal, but on a large screen in a dark space, the effect of direct address is still profound. It creates a remarkable intimacy, a claim to honesty, an intimation of confession, of baring the soul (even when the actual message contradicts this), and an immediacy or present-ness. The combination of the present-ness with our knowledge of the historical context of the films, as well as their status as early soldiers' self-representation, give them a powerful aesthetic effect, but some of the anonymous film directors in Burma struggled to combine this with a quasi-fictional world where the soldiers remained seemingly unaware of the camera.

These experiments in the integration of the new form with an objective camera view were perhaps attempted to make sense of the innovation. Thus, in another film three men on a bench barter with an Indian employee to buy a pen: '10 chips (rupees)'. The response is 'I'll offer you five' and then a voice from behind the camera asks 'hello what do you want a pen for?'. 'I'd like to write the weekly letter home.' 'Well would you like to skip it this week?' After the messages are delivered, this little scene also has a coda, as the soldier hands the pen, now reduced to 8 chips, back to the salesman – 'Here you are John, there's no need for this now' (*CB* 380 1946). Other sequences feature prologues involving motor transport; in

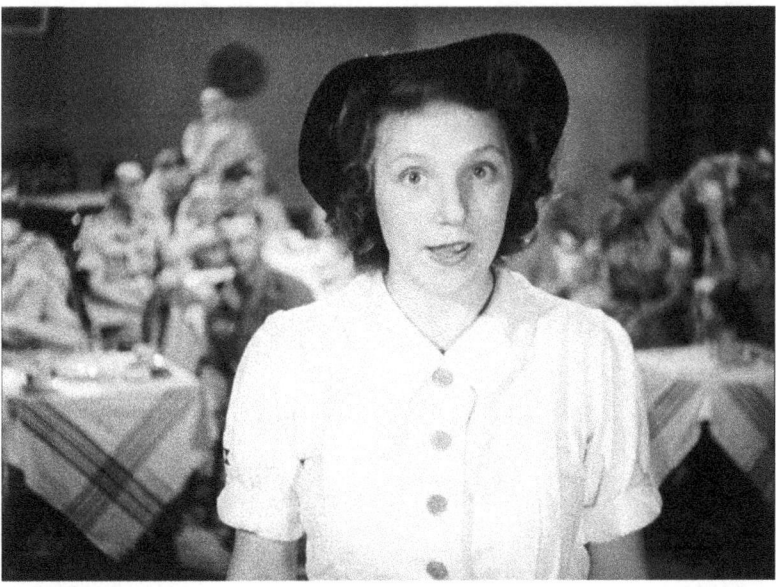

FIGURE 4.9: Betty Hedge, one of the few women who appear in the films (*CB* 52 1944). © IWM.

one a motorcyclist revs up his engine but immediately switches it off to speak his message (*CB* 191 1945). A group of men clustered around the open bonnet of a lorry engage in banter before the voice of authority asks them if they want to send a greeting. 'If you put a new engine in it, it might go. Aye and if you get your shirt off and started sweating a bit we might have a better chance' (*CB* 183 1945). Jarring though these sequences are, they do give some insight into everyday lives of the soldiers, apart from actual warfare of course, which otherwise remains absent from the films. Unusually, in some sequences, the apparatus of filmmaking is shown directly, as well as referred to. So that in one sequence a group of men rush up to an officer in the grounds of the studios apparently in a hurry, supposedly as their late for the film. 'This is *Calling Blighty*, but you're a bit late aren't you?'. One answers 'We were detained on the road'. The senior officer says 'I wonder if we've packed up yet? Have we packed up yet Lance?'. The cameramen shouts that they are still running and the mic is brought into shot so that the men can turn around, as they are told to, and address the camera (*CB* 219 1945).

In another episode, we see the whole camera crew, filming a message that we have previously watched, where a group of men clustered around a radio set switch it off, and one delivers a moving message about the death of his mother. This is a revealing insight into the film process. A group of men walk up and feign innocent

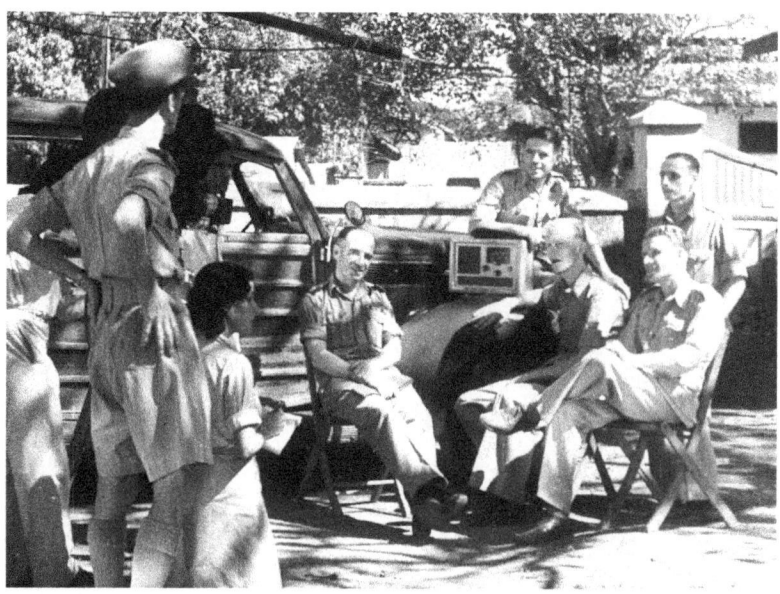

FIGURE 4.10: Film within a film, Central Studios Bombay (*CB* 273 1946). © IWM.

enquiry – 'What's going on here then?'. The director tells them to keep quiet and shouts for the crew to cut. As well as the camera and cameraman and director, we also see an Indian woman kneeling in uniform with a notepad, one of the rare portrayals of the empire troops in all the surviving *Blighty* films and an equally rare depiction of a woman at all in the largely masculine world of the films (*CB* 273 1946). Again 'the purpose of this meta-film is unclear, apart from the rather weak introduction to the group of men; "These men are sending messages home from Manchester"'. 'Well we're from Manchester!'. Although equally stretching of credulity, it works rather better than the letter writing sequences, as the glimpse of the filmmaking setup is still interesting now and must have held no little interest for the families seeing the film in their home cinema.

The methods of ending the films were varied and ranged from the elaborate, and the musical, to extremely simple. For the films made in the studio in Bombay, these were often accompanied by apparently live music in the background (although sometimes also recorded popular music), played by Harry Allen, a skilful pianist, who often played an extended piece on the piano to conclude, surrounded by the men and women who had just delivered their messages. These performances such as Jungle Swing were in the then-contemporary boogie-woogie or swing style and were highly energetic and indeed virtuoso exhibitions. Other endings were more downbeat, a small group of men waving goodbye and walking towards the sea, or jumping in the back of a lorry which then drove off. Many films ended with men singing a popular song strongly connected to their city or region: 'On Ilkley Moor Baht 'at', for the South Yorkshire men, 'We Are the Leicester boys', 'A Lassie From Lancashire', or 'Sailing Down the Clyde'. These regional songs, sung both in the studio and in the battle zones in Burma, strongly reinforced the localized identity of the groups of men.

Many men spoke with strong local accents, but there is a wide variety, and especially among the officers in the films more middle-class tones can be heard side by side with Oldham or Norfolk accents. This was unusual in wartime film. Audiences in the 1940s heard accents that were perceived as classless if they were Hollywood American, but strongly divided on class lines if they were British. Rattigan observes that the class-based society that existed in Britain on rigid social and cultural lines is reflected in the British films produced during the war – the upper-class nature of leadership as revealed by incidental detail and especially the public-school accents of the senior officer characters (Rattigan 2001: 267). The men in the films speak within a prescribed format but spontaneously, in their original accents, possibly for the first time ever in British film. It was the case that the Northern and especially the Lancastrian voice was seen up until the 1940s and beyond as something essentially comic, as exemplified by George Formby, Gracie Fields, Jimmy Clitheroe and Frank Randle. Randle and Formby were particularly successful in wartime and the former had a string of low-budget slapstick comedies such as *Somewhere in Camp* and *Somewhere on Leave*, both in 1942 (Aldgate and Richards 1986: 89). Jo Fox (2006: 820) asserts that in wartime it was the documentary movement that 'gave cinematic identity to the popular conception of class, regional, and gender constructs' and that the use of accents and language was one of the key devices in this construction. The regional voice was reserved for non-serious subjects, and the metropolitan upper-class accent was still consistently invoked for documentary voice-overs, newsreels, or anything requiring critical depth. The men speaking in the *Blighty* films in their Rochdale or Salford accents are presented in a warm but serious context, which adds to their authenticity and immediacy to the viewer today. Within the frame of the *Blighty* film and the censorship of wartime, they represent themselves, and these are self-portraits rather than highly mediated representations through the often patronizing filter of pre- and post-war non-fiction film.

Part of the significance of the *Blighty* films lies within their recording of the self-presentation of working men (and women), especially outside London, at a time when the self-authored statement on film, with its occasional guilelessness and hesitancy, was extremely rare. Elizabeth Sussex suggests (Sussex 1975: 42) that in pre-war documentary and John Grierson's *Drifters* (1929) in particular, the workers depicted are 'shown from what today would be regarded as a middle-class establishment viewpoint. In the *Calling Blighty* films, we do get close to working people as people, albeit in an artificial situation, and where the content of what they say is less important than the fact that they filmed saying it and are seen by their relatives.

The 1935 film *Housing Problems* made by Edgar Anstey (with the significant help of Ruby Grierson, especially with the interviews) was the first documentary in which working-class voices of East End men and women could be heard, but they seem to us stilted or to be following a script. But as John Corner has pointed out the voices in *Housing Problems* are more properly regarded as 'a form of mediated public speaking' than the kind of naturalistic and informal interview that we are used to today. This is also the case with the *Blighty* voices, which also represent 'a self-authored statement to the viewer (an '"access" message')' (Corner 1996: 68) with all the awkwardness and often stilted demeanour that is absent from contemporary filmic interviews. Rather than see this as inauthentic, Corner suggests that this is a 'guarantee of communicative honesty' (Corner 1996: 68), as people who have no experience at all of speaking to the camera and probably little of public speaking of any kind address the lens (and by implication their loved ones) and are then viewed in the powerfully intimate and dark confines of the cinema. The illusion of naturalism is a false expectation.

Heart of Britain, the famous documentary made by Humphrey Jennings in 1941, has a section in which Sheffield steelworker George Good speaks in a seemingly off-the-cuff way, but his performance is 'painfully self-conscious, addressing his lines to an off-camera director' (Smith 2003: 138). His delivery is a world away from Lieutenant Corporal Wilf Parker, the Sheffield man who appears in a *Calling Blighty* film three years later speaking from a golf course in Bombay, whose accent is instantly recognisable in North Sheffield today, speaking to his brother. 'Hiya our kid' (*CB* 252 1946). Issues of class and regionality are challenged by the *Blighty* films, but also in some ways reinforced. There is a hierarchy of rank seen on and off-screen; the director and welfare officer involved in the filming were Captains, with the remaining film crew drawn from the lower ranks of Lieutenants, Warrant Officers and Sergeants. But through these filters of military hierarchy and the dominance of the pre-war class system, we see on screen an authentic working-class voice, pre-echoes of an approach that did not become accepted in popular cinema until the kitchen sink, British new wave films of the late 1950s.

5

Masculinity and the Soldier's Tale

If by some magic we were together I'd tell you quietly all that I cannot tell you in a letter. [...] But [the fundamental unchanging things] sing out in my heart like a branch of cherries and seven singing dwarfs, louder than all the trumpets, and it's the only true meaning in the sunshine in the scene.

(Poet Alun Lewis's last letter to his wife Gweno from Burma in 1944 [Lewis 1946: 424])

The men in the *Calling Blighty* films struggle to express themselves, in an unfamiliar and sometimes uncomfortable medium, one they only know from the seats in the stalls of the Regal Twins, Manchester or the Haymarket, Norwich. The stiff upper lip of wartime Britain is overlaid with something more revealing of their masculinity; they were finding their own ways of portraying themselves, with no previous models to rely on. Borrowing from familiar tropes, written post cards, snatches of popular song, ironic comparisons with well-known film stars and a shorthand of contemporary greetings – keep smiling and keep your chin up, I'm in the pink – they manage to also speak in their authentic voices. Having volunteered and being chosen to deliver a message, a rare privilege and the first men in history to do so in film, they were faced with having to choose the expression of their masculinity in wartime, speaking from a far distant theatre unimaginable to their audience. Am I the family man, the warrior hero, the responsible son or the flippant joker of the pack? Do I remember my community, emphasize my regional roots, give away the reality of my war against an implacable enemy, and can I express the powerful bond I have with my comrades, my division?

Despite all this uncertainty, the men manage to transcend the hurdles of class and awkwardness in a way that still resonates powerfully today. These films present the first filmed messages of a large body of men and a handful of women, from the theatre of war. They are remarkable for their portrayal of masculinity in wartime, however, constrained by the format and the unseen shadow of military authority behind the camera, but they form part of a long history of soldiers' letters and self-representation going back millennia.

One of the earliest existing letters from a serving soldier is the 1800-year-old papyrus written by Aurelius Polion, an Egyptian soldier serving in a Roman Legion in Europe, possibly Aquincum, the present-day Budapest. His letter written in Greek to his brother, sister and mother 'the bread seller' shows striking similarities to the concerns of the men in the *Blighty* films. In particular, he is concerned about the absence of regular mail – he has sent six letters that have gone unanswered – 'I do not cease writing to you, but you do not have me in mind [...]. You never wrote to me concerning your health, how you are doing'. He is also anxious to get home leave, something the men of the 14th Army knew was almost impossible for them: 'The moment you have me in mind, I shall obtain leave from the consular (senior officer) and I shall come to you so that you may know that I am your brother'. The longing for a distant home is a universally held soldier's concern, but there are other factors at play. Aurelius was literate, much rarer then than it is now, and a lack of literacy handicapped the majority of British soldiers until the late Victorian era. Aurelius was also exceptional in that he was multilingual and could probably also write in Egyptian and Latin, although as with other historical military letters his handwriting, spelling and grammar are erratic (Ruth-Rice 2014: n.pag.).

An even earlier eyewitness account of war goes almost back to the beginnings of war itself when the military scribe Tjaneni (or Thanuny c.1455 BCE) accompanied Thutmose the Third on a campaign to put down a revolt in Egypt. The battle of Meggido took place 3500 years ago but Tjaneni's account of it, which Thutmose evidently enjoyed so much he had it inscribed on the temple walls at Amun, shows in its triumphal tone features recognizable in contemporary accounts from victorious soldiers. The rebel Kadesh is reviled, always referred to as 'the wretched enemy', and there is much jubilant detailing of the spoils of war, slaves and golden artefacts, wrested from the defeated opponent (Mark 2009: n.pag.).

The soldiers in the World War II films probably had high levels of literacy, certainly compared to most periods of history, but the recent innovation of synchronized sound on film meant that their messages could be spoken, rendering the ability to write irrelevant. But in Victorian times, apart from home leave, the letter was the only way of reaching out to home and family, and levels of literacy in the non-officer class were much lower. Forster's education act of 1870 had provided a framework for elementary education, but before this the ability to read and write in the army was by no means widespread. Illiteracy, in the sense of being unable to write one's own name, was said to be 90 per cent in the ranks in 1860, but the army instituted its own certificate of education as a condition of promotion, and by 1878, nearly 50 per cent were regarded as possessing a 'superior level of education'. Ten years later this had grown to 85% and by the Anglo-Zulu War of 1879 it was said that letter writing was the main relaxation of the men in their encampments (Spiers 2018: 2).

Some of the letters written from the front in the late Victorian era had strong literary and journalistic merit, and many were in fact regularly published in national and regional newspapers as contemporary war reporting. By the South African (Boer) War, this was so common that men sent letters directly for publication, sometimes anonymously, in the 'Letters from the front' columns of the newspapers. Often these had a highly local dimension, foreshadowing the *Calling Blighty* films in their tightly bound amalgam of region and war – 'A Wiganer in South Africa', 'Letters from Bury lads', or 'A Pitlochry soldier's baptism of fire' (Spiers 2018: n.pag.). One soldier who wrote regularly from the Sudan was Winston Churchill, who was incidentally paid quite well at £10 per column. But while some of these letters have vivid accounts of hand-to-hand fighting, with a desire to engage their foes (echoes of the 'wretched enemy' of 1500 BC) and to gain revenge for fallen comrades, other letter writers struggled to find their appropriate voice.

In the sepoy letters of the Great War, selected for publication by David Omissi, the soldiers showed similarities with the men of the 14th Army on film 30 years later. Despite the fact that they were writing to friends and family at home and not for publication to a public conditioned to expect an arduous but ultimately triumphal narrative, they tended to express a degree of self-censorship. The letters, often written through scribes, as many of the sepoys were illiterate, had often a 'somewhat stilted and conformist prose, reflecting either standard phrases [...] or the inhibitions of the author as he expressed himself in a semi-public arena' (Omissi cited in Spiers 2018: n.pag.). Ironically, the Victorian soldiers were probably much freer of ostensible censorship at regimental or more senior levels than many twentieth century correspondents or the men in the *Calling Blighty* films. Whilst the films are ostensibly free of censorship, every serviceman would have known instinctively what could and what could not be said, even if they could ignore the gaze of the welfare officer and the other higher ranks behind the camera. They were also highly conditioned by the very public nature of the declarations to their loved ones back home, and the brief format left little time to say much except to reassure and demonstrate that they were well and thinking of their relatives.

Jay Winter (Winter 2006: 104) considers Philipp Witkop's post-World War I celebrated collection of the letters of fallen German soldiers, filtered through Witkop's own national view, showing these men as both aware of their war and its evils, and also expressing a romantic and sentimental viewpoint. He notes that censorship operated in respect of these letters on many levels: 'Soldiers were well aware of the Army censor's sensibilities and may have limited their griping or caustic remarks accordingly. In addition there is the censorship of the men themselves with respect to their families' sensibilities' (Winter 2006: 110). This is also apparent in the *Blighty* messages.

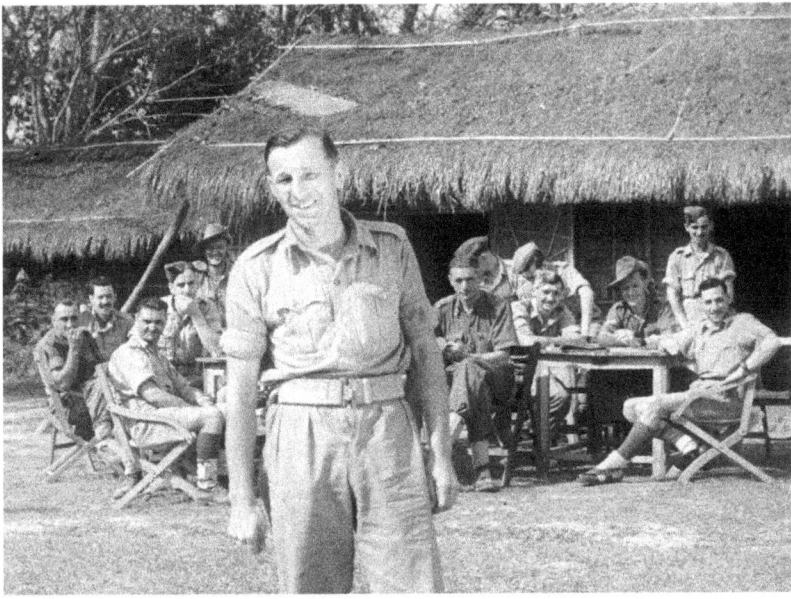

FIGURE 5.1: South Yorkshire men. 'I'll be coming home soon, then we'll have a real good time together' (*CB* Yorkshire 1945). © Yorkshire Film Archive.

In terms of references to war, none of the remaining films shows any overt action, but several show the paraphernalia of war, the sights and sounds and the men within it. In one film of men from York filmed in Burma, their messages are delivered to the background sound of explosions, and there is an ironic riposte to a man who says he will be home soon, as the men behind him say to much laughter 'You hope' (*CB* 1945). In a film of Brighton men from 1945 'Mike' says 'All of us boys here are going to win the war and get back to you a bit jolly' (*CB* 151 1945). And as noted the films made just after the fall of Mandalay are the closest to overt war films. Winter suggests of World War I memoirs that they fortify a view as both noble and uplifting, but this is much less apparent in the *Calling Blighty* films, where the men hardly express any opinions about the war they are engaged in, focusing instead on the here and now, the regularity of the mail, the visible health and demeanour of the speaker.

The men in these films deliver 'self-authored statements' in John Corner's formulation, rather than off-the-cuff informality. Despite being in a brutal conflict, almost none depict themselves as warrior heroes. Partly this was the nature of men in World War II, at least in relation to their families, where loss and heroism were understated, a stoic acceptance seen also in contemporary films such as *Mrs Miniver*. There is an acknowledgement of friends and relations who are also in the services. Some films are punctuated by machine gun fire and explosions, as in the film of Leicester men in Burma (*CB* 155 1945), but more often the response to the conflict is ironic: 'Remember Tojo can't beat a man who's served his time on t'corporation bus', says a Lancashire man in Burma in a broad regional accent (*CB* 132 1945).

Some men found their orientation of expression in references to familiar film stars or snatches of popular song, a series of shortcuts to their acknowledgement of the unfamiliar situation. 'I know I'm not much of a film actor' (*CB* 1945). Walter Penfold from Brighton (*CB* 285 1946) says 'I guess this is the first and last chance I will have to rival Don Ameche'. Some men quote popular comedians – 'Cooey, you lucky people!', from Tommy Trinder's famous catchphrase, or song titles: 'Hi good looking, what's cooking?' (*CB* 1945). Or a man from Wolverhampton, 'In any case, in the words of the popular song; I love you truly' (*CB* 1944). It is as if the borrowed, if well-worn phrases provide a distance to enable the utterance of what is too close to the heart to be said. Other men allowed signs of vulnerability to be revealed, in their words or appearance. 'And you know, everything is going, well you know so-so' (*CB* 41 1944). From a man who appears nervous, his eye twitching: 'Don't worry about me, I'm fine. Life in India isn't too bad but I miss you an awful lot' (*CB* 41 1944). There are references to illness and injury: 'I've

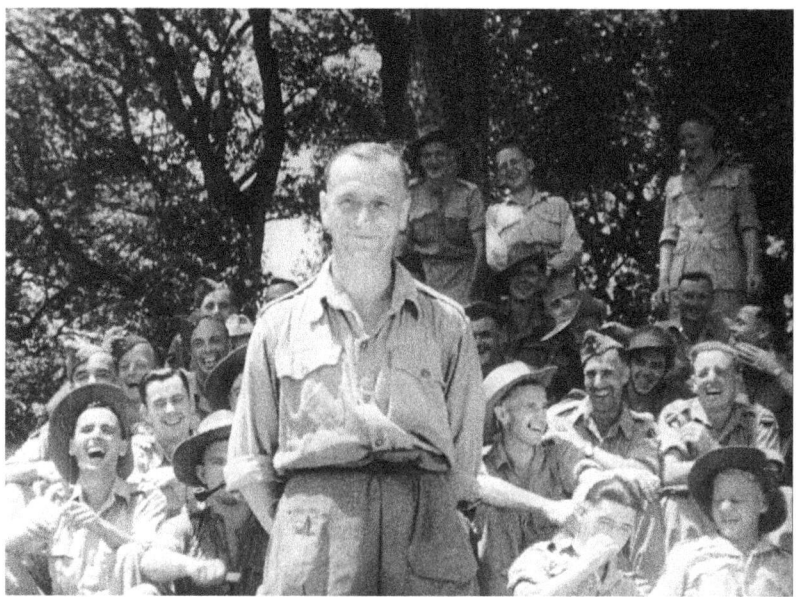

FIGURE 5.2: 'And remember, Tojo can't shake a man who's served his time on t'Corporation Bus' (*CB* 132 1945). © IWM.

just come out of hospital – as you can see I'm fit and well' (*CB* 205 1945). 'I'm not feeling too bad after the accident' (*CB* 86 1944). 'I expect you'll be thinking how thin I look; well it's only to be expected in these hot countries' (*CB* 86 1944). 'I hope you're not too shocked at how much I've changed' (*CB* 206 1945).

Others express positive sentiments but seem to belie this in their appearance. 'Hello Nora darling, I am fine as you can see', a message delivered from soldier with a distinctly haunted look on his face (*CB* 311 1946). Others deliver their messages wearing a uniform that is drenched in sweat. Many find the whole thing uncomfortable – 'It's very awkward here in front of the camera, knowing exactly what to say' (*CB* 354 1946). 'What else was I going to say Frank, I'm blowed if I can remember?' ('You'll be home soon' he is prompted by his comrade) (*CB* 391 1946). For some the yearning for home and loved ones is almost tangible: 'This morning I was looking into the Irrawaddy, and I could see you all in my imagination, as plain as you can see me now' (*CB* 206 1945). Frank from Worcester is one of several who speak to the children they have never seen: 'Well son, this is the first time you've ever seen me, or heard me talk. Soon I hope to be with you, taking you fishing and all those things you want me to do (*CB* 56 1944)'. And a Sheffield man hopes that 'Sheila is not too disappointed to see her daddy for the first time' (*CB* 86 1944).

The exposed and very public nature of the cinema meant that any overt reference to sexuality was almost absent, certainly compared to the privacy of conventional mail, but there are hints of what could not be said. 'You know what I would say if all these people weren't listening and looking' (*CB* 89 1944). However, some men did allow themselves to express some negative emotions despite the relentless chin-up morale building. 'Everything is well over here, I'm having a good time. I hope to be home soon though, I'm a bit browned off with this country' (*CB* 387 1946). 'There are some lovely places in India; of course this isn't one of them' (*CB* 199 1945). There are hints of unresolved troubles and emotional as well as physical distance. 'Mail depressing from your area; I don't know what's gone wrong' (*CB* 1945). 'I don't know what you mean by Bill being in the army; I haven't heard nothing of it' (*CB* 1944). And from Benny Collison of Brighton to his wife back home: 'Reference our little bit of trouble, forget it. I shall ascribe everything when I come home' (*CB* 89 1944).

But far more numerous were messages of hope, looking forward to the end of the war, and the peaceful future beyond it. 'Hello Walsall, pleased to know the poultry farm is doing okay. You better save a couple for me when I come home' (*CB* 1945). A Brighton man to his wife, 'I hope it won't be long before we're all back together again and having some lox and soup on Fridays' (*CB* 89 1944). Frank from Norwich enthuses 'It's good to know our home is being rebuilt. I'll be round to see you one of these days' (*CB* 50 1944). 'Let's get this job over soon and we'll be back together' (*CB* 57 1944). 'Get the fatted calf in and plenty of beers' (*CB* 56 1944). And a Manchester man obviously struggling to control his emotion says 'Hello Sis darling; miss you very much darling. Keep smiling and remember I miss you more than anything else in the world' (*CB* 58 1944).

Thumim talks of a 'genre of self-representation', because of the repeated characteristics when such representations appear, which allows us to decode the values within a set of generic conventions. We expect to see and hear something in the contemporary era of self-representation that is truthful and authentic; these elements include ordinary people, experience, emotion, a personal journey, speaking to the camera in close up and interior worlds. The *Blighty* films embody many of these specifics, and they have some aspects that do seem direct and authentic, but they have to be viewed through the mediation of Thumim's three dimensions, institutional processes and textual and cultural filters that condition how we view the films (and how they were viewed at the time) (Thumim 2012: 166).

It is possible to compare the experiences of one soldier in Burma not only through his writing but also the images he created of India and Burma, through the collected letters, paintings and photographs of James Fenton, a 20-year-old from Oswaldtwistle, Lancashire, who was called up in 1942 after studying at the local art school, which he combined with sentry duty in the Local Defence Volunteers, later the Home Guard. Fenton was a prolific and eloquent letter writer to his parents back in Lancashire as well as his brother Harry and later his wife Lilian, but he was also a talented artist who later made a successful career as a freelance creative artist and graphic designer. His written and visual impressions of the conflict give an interesting counterpoint to the films, showing what could be said and depicted, as he saw action first on the Arakan coast and later chasing the Japanese forces down through Burma, as a gunner or signaller and driver with the Royal Artillery in the 36th Division.

As he points out, strict censorship regulations on leaving England 'prohibited the disclosure of troop ships, military activities, locations and place names, or information that may be of value to the enemy', and hostile encounters with the Japanese could not be reported until almost the end of the war (Fenton 2012: foreword). Letters had to pass the censor and often orders changed, as to what they could and could not write home about; hence they often reached home with passages blocked out. After restrictions on the use of unofficial cameras by front-line fighting units were relaxed, as the defeat of the Japanese became inevitable, he managed to get by January 1945 his Zonal Junior folding plate camera sent to him via family friends who lived in India, along with chemicals and photographic paper. Despite the tropical heat and being frequently under fire from Japanese guns, he managed to take numerous photographs of the indigenous people and places in Burma, to supplement the many sketches and paintings that he had made throughout the war.

As in the films, the letters range over a variety of concerns with comparatively little focusing on overt action, which censorship meant was difficult to record in any case. The difficulties and practicalities of sending and receiving mail, and even of the act of writing, as ink dries out on his pen nib in the intense heat, making it difficult to write, are frequently mentioned, along with food and drink, illness and its treatment, the infrequent entertainment, the monsoon and skilfully drawn pen portraits of the landscape and the boredom of military training. Fenton from these letters has an optimistic if pragmatic disposition; like most of the men in the films, he accepts the privations of his lot and looks forward to the future. It is telling that his period in Burma came just as the tide of war was turning, with the incursion into Arakan in which he took part, and the Japanese defeat at Kohima/Imphal, in which his Division was not involved, followed by pursuit of the enemy down through Burma from November 1944 onwards. Unlike many of his fellow soldiers, he had an intense visual curiosity about the country and its people, and his vivid impressions seem to have spurred him on in the long months and years of active service.

His paintings and drawings reflect a realistic portrayal of the life of a soldier in India and Burma. There are portraits of local children, landscape scenes and depictions of the soldiers of other nationalities he was fighting alongside, images that are noticeably absent from the *Calling Blighty* films. But there are also pictures of military life, a still life of a survival kit, or equipment captured by the Japanese, a soldier reading in a dugout or writing a letter home by the light of Tilley lamp. There are even scenes witnessed during fighting, 'sketched in sepia from memory, I produced in calm moments between sudden interruptions from our unsociable enemy'. These included crossing the Shweli River at Myitson, and vivid impressions of action attacking the same city, and the 3.7 howitzers laying down a barrage attacking Pinwe. Many of these extraordinary images, the kind absent from the *Blighty* films for obvious reasons, were sent for publication to England during the war.

In his written descriptions of action, there were differences in what could be said and what could not be said, sometimes because of the censor, but also due to his desire to spare his parents from worry. Six months after the event, he says about his 'worst day ever', 15 February 1945, at Myitson: 'My nerves were affected by Japanese artillery constantly shelling our position at night [...] we worked to exhaustion before nightfall digging a slit trench for defence'. 'We needed no encouragement [...] if we wished to survive another day'. What he did not write at the time was an experience checking a box of hand grenades at night, which he noticed had suffered corrosion in the humidity. He tested the split pin to see whether it would still withdraw whilst holding the firing pin down with his left hand, but in the dark was unable to get the pin back in. 'Nerves in sweaty hands complicated the task', and he could not throw the grenade for fear of alerting the Japanese. He eventually tied the pin down with his leather boot laces and hoped it would survive intact until daylight, when he replaced the pin (Fenton 2012: 113). To disclose this in a letter could have led to a court martial, as well as worrying his parents, and there must have been countless similar situations in the war for the tens of thousands of British troops. All are absent from the films. At occasional dances when not in action, apart from a few women of the FANY (First Aid Nursing Yeomanry), there was a distinct absence of female partners. Fenton commented 'I had a great time as can be expected, even if the night is spent dancing with one of the guys. With few girls around this is the only way many lads can enjoy dancing' (Fenton 2012: 196).

Three months after delivering his filmed message to his parents for the *Calling Blighty* cameras at the Shree studios in Bombay, Tag Barnes from Sheffield was at the Arakan. Having pushed the Japanese back from the Myebon peninsular, they were detached to make a potentially dangerous search of a large island that lay at the fork of the river at the head of the peninsula, to see whether there were any Japanese in occupation, and he wrote some weeks later to his father with an accounts of the reconnaissance. Tag's filmed message had been laconic in the extreme; cigarette in hand he apologizes for not being home for an anniversary but hopes he will next year' (*CB* 86 1944). He introduces the next man on film, a rather portly soldier to his wife Mrs Scott and jokes that 'He doesn't seem to be doing so bad on the bully beef'. But the letter shines a different light on both the kind of hazardous operations he underwent, even before he won the military medal in a later battle in the Arakan but also his state of mind when in action.

On the landing craft to the island the twelve men settle down, 'Each of us in his own mind wondering whether we should ever see another magnificent sunset'. He stands in the boat looking into the water and 'I noticed I was not the only one staring over the gunnels; Four tight-lipped, grim faced Royal Indian Naval officers each one cuddling a Lewis machine gun under his armpit were scanning the black undergrowth'. The sortie starts badly as the boat runs aground in the dark with a crash: 'Good lord I thought, and they must have heard us in Tokyo'. 'My goodness Dad it was quiet, [...] I could almost hear my heart beating. With every nerve tense and tingling, for a few moments one lived in another world' (Barnes 1991: 91).

They stagger ashore 'thigh deep into black stinking mud' and climb up the jungle in the night-time tropical heat where they keep watch. 'Thus Dad, we spent the night (as we have spent many nights) watching, listening, aching for want of sleep, thinking of you at home and praying for the dawn'. When light comes, they establish that no enemy are present on the hill then move on by compass bearing to the next one: 'We couldn't even see the hill, you can never see much in virgin jungle, not even the sky. One relies entirely on compass bearings'. But at 10:30 a.m., their water bottle is empty and already due to perspiration and humidity and heat having developed a severe thirst, they find that a stream marked on their map was bone dry. They realize the Japanese had no interest in the island, 'The absence of water was undoubtedly the reason'. This was their seventh consecutive day without sleep but eventually they find a pool in a stream bed after sliding down an almost vertical slope clinging to vines to break their fall. 'The last hope of quenching our now intense thirst'. To their horror the water was salty, it was a pool left by the ebbing tidal river. They discover a cup full of stale sweet water caught in the bowl of a tree. 'For five minutes we stood around it dipping in our fingers, and moistening our lips. All this seemed to do was enrage our thirst a hundredfold'. Finally they reach the mangrove swamp and their landing craft arrives, where 'water was dished out in mess tins [...] I shall never forget that first drink. Never had I tasted anything so sweet. Nectar Of the gods' (Barnes 1991: 95).

Barnes muses that if their sortie were reported in the papers it would probably read 'Patrol reconnaissance on Arakan Island. The patrol met no opposition' and reflects on the gulf between such a bald description and the ordeal they had (willingly) gone through. But the gulf between the public presentation of consolation in the *Calling Blighty* films and the day-to-day reality of jungle warfare for those who engaged in it was equally huge, eloquently outlined in Barnes's moving account.

Such honesty about the real conditions is necessarily absent from the films, but there is within them an ironic voice that 'stands with suspicion towards pompous rhetoric' (Choularaki 2016: 59). Flying Officer Timmins in Burma, with grim humour and in Lancashire dialect (he uses the word 'gradely' meaning 'excellent'), refers to the possibility of death. 'This film comes to you by courtesy of the bully beef, beans, and browned-off tea corporation, showing you some of Britain's bonny boys stationed in Burma. Of course folks you have seen Hedy Lamarr with Charles Boyer, you've seen Dorothy Lamour, in, and out of her sarong, you have seen Betty Grable with the twinkling legs, but you have seen nothing yet until you have seen the stars in the green battledress. Eee, it's a real gradely place, a real gradely place for anybody, to *die* in' (his companions laugh) (*CB* 210 1945). This ironic voice is different to Witkop's German messages. As Winter notes (2006: 116), there is some scepticism about the nature of a universal soldier's tale, and the Northern and Mancunian voice here expresses particular inflections and references, which 'disclose a cultural memory, a national archive of meanings which are not the same as those linked to other national groups' (2006: 117).

In the same film, a sequence follows where marching paratroopers sing 'Blood on the Risers', the traditional parachute regiment song, to the tune of John Brown's

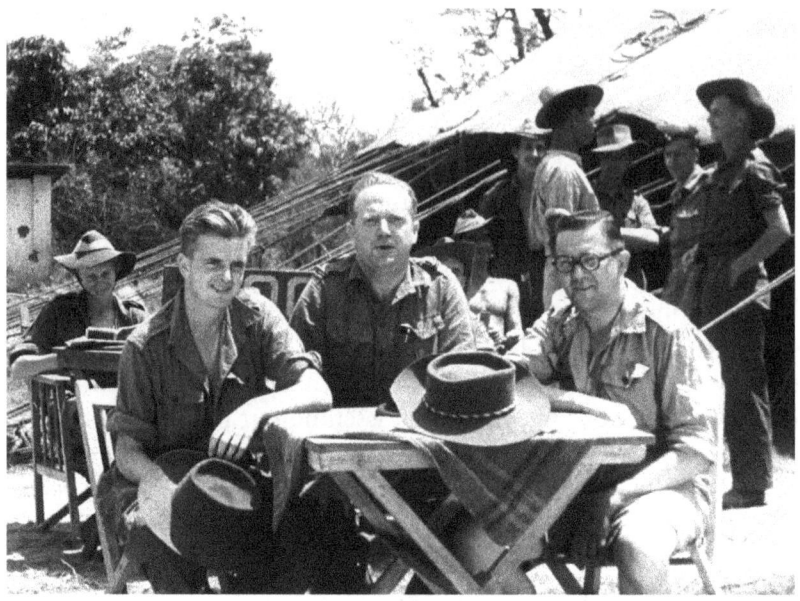

FIGURE 5.3: Flying Officer Timmins, 'a gradely place to die in' (*CB* 210 1945). © IWM.

body. 'Glory Glory what a hell of a way to die, and we ain't gonna jump no more' (*CB* 210 1945). These are almost the only references to death and the very real risks of combat in the films – in fact some 27,000 Anglo-Indian troops died of injury or disease in India and Burma (McLynn 2011: 1). The real war can be heard in several of the films as explosions or gunfire offscreen, but in their utterances the men only reference death with a twinkle in the eye and an ironic pride in the risks to them and their comrades.

Keggie Carew wrote about her father's heroic wartime experiences and contrasted them with his inability to accommodate to peacetime normality. Tom Carew had been a wartime hero, a member of the Jedburghs, the elite force within a force that was part of the Special Operations Executive (SOE), where he won the DSO, and was characterized at the time in a *Times of India* article as 'Lawrence of Burma'. The article went on to say he was 'a secret service agent who has organized guerilla bands of natives to harass Jap lines of communications and send intelligence reports to British commanders; his name cannot yet be revealed'. Carew's personality was fitted for wartime; his radio operator in Burma, John Sharp, describes him as 'Let's say he was, adventurous. Well he was brave to the point of [...]'. 'Stupidity?'. 'Let's say just had no fear at all. He wasn't like any officer I'd met before' (Carew 2016: 153).

Just before being parachuted into the Arakan in December 1944 to begin the mission referred to in the *Times of India*, he wrote to his parents. Typically reflecting the attitude of the *Calling Blighty* messages, after chatting about the heat and the advantages of bush shorts over tropical shorts, he disarmingly apologises for the future level of contact. 'My letter writing will lapse [...] as I will be rushing around all over the place and working rather hard. Your loving son, Arthur' (Carew 2016: 152). His unit, co-named Camel, successfully recruited an armed Arakanese guerilla force against the Japanese, despite numerous opponents ranged against them, not only the enemy but the military wing of the British Burmese government in exile, the CAS(B), who rightly feared that an armed Burmese nationalist force would not only want to throw out the invaders but also the pre-war colonial occupiers as well. Camel's operation was a great success – the guerrillas accounted for 4200 enemy killed, the enemy was driven out of the Arakan, and the key airfield at a Akyab was back in Allied use, from where bombers could attack Rangoon. The victory was attributed in Mountbatten's base in Ceylon to the 'personal courage, coolness and resourcefulness of Major Carew'. His swashbuckling wartime exploits as he acknowledges himself in a letter home were 'More romantic than a Rafael Sabatini novel, and unbelievably successful. I shall tell you all about it one day' (Carew 2016: 172).

However, Tom Carew's 'fearless' heroism by any standards translated badly into post-war Britain and the realities of employment and family. In the introduction to Robert Taylor's *Wartime Traveller*, he compares Carew to the greats of Burmese wartime mythology: 'Many have read of the exploits of Merrill's Marauders and Wingate's Chindits, but few will ever know of the adventures of Major Tom Carew or Thakin Tin Shwe, the Burmese 'freedom fighter'. But the masculine values he embodied so well in war, thrived afterwards at first in Trieste and Gibraltar, in an expat life in the army of sailing and extravagant parties, but then in 1958, his young family fly back to 'a cold grey jobless, post-war Britain'. He considers farming or running a grocery shop but without capital they prove impracticable. He opens a boat yard instead with borrowed family money, but it founders in three years in a mountain of debt, after which he looks for work all over the country, where there is however 'no call for guerrilla agents in Fareham'. 'Money was just around the corner, one more plan, one more venture, one more more' (Carew 2016: 277). Family relationships fracture and his wife suffers from mental illness; they divorce. His situation was by no means unusual in Britain after the war. Jack Greasley who appeared in *Calling Blighty* 203 and his wife had good jobs and a comfortable lifestyle before the war, but when he came back from India they both found it very difficult. They struggled to find work and lived on the breadline. He retrained as a painter and decorator under a Government training scheme for a housing boom that did not materialize and was again unemployed, until eventually he did find work, although with a tied cottage. This was even more pointed as their siblings who had not fought were doing extremely well. Two who were too old to be called up ran successful businesses and one who was a conscientious objector became manager of a cotton mill (Greasley 2020).

Not all the men serving in Burma expressed the same reckless bravado. The poet Alun Lewis, from south Wales, enlisted in the Royal Engineers in 1940, despite being a pacifist, and after service in India was moved to the Arakan. He was a gifted writer, and his 1942 collection *Raider's Dawn and other Poems*, established him as one of the outstanding war poets. In it, he describes the loneliness of military life and the effect that new postings had on him; his volume of short stories, *The Last Inspection*, published the same year, was equally powerful. But he also wrote an illuminating and powerfully honest series of letters to his wife Gweno who he had married just before embarkation, in July 1941.

He had joined the Royal Engineers in the ranks despite his pacifism to help defeat fascism but then inexplicably decided to pursue a commission in an infantry battalion. The change of path was not a success. It was said of his poems that they showed 'His brooding over his army experiences and trying to catch and hold some vision that would illuminate its desolation with meaning' (Wikipedia 2020: n.pag.). His letters show that as an officer his duties were varied. 'This evening I'll be censoring letters and putting on a gramophone recital in the reading room' (Lewis 1989: 405), and he sought rare solitude and solace swimming in a nearby lake. 'I swam in leisurely as the dusk grew and came back with a lovely bodily feeling of being well and balanced on the Earth' (Lewis 1989: 406). But there are intimations of depression: 'I wish they'd leave Christmas alone, I don't want it. I simply want to clear my head of the darkness that has gathered there like water in a swamp'. He openly makes clear his need for Gweno's letters from home in a way that the men in the *Blighty* films could not. She 'ministered (her) warmth and careful love to me in the way that unmans me because it's such a different world from the coarse swearing, ranting, violent atmosphere that has come into being in the battalion and in the mess' (Lewis 1989: 409).

His heart had 'grown a crust so that I can't break it but it leaves my body leaderless'. A Christmas hymn breaks through the hard shell and 'my eyes began to sob and something tender that I've been hiding, hiding even from myself, woke for a minute and wept'. His response to the harsh war was conditioned by his sensitivity and leads to being 'downcast and bedraggled of soul. I feel I'm being true to the realities in feeling this way; India is really a great purgatory and so is the war, and so is the future we are facing'. He wrote his last letter home on February 20th, 1944: 'The darkness and threats are from another part of ourselves. And the long self-torture I've been through is resolving itself into a discipline of the emotions' (Lewis 1989: 424) 'I feel my grasp is broader and steadier than it has been for a long time. I hope it's true, because that's how I want it to be' (Lewis 1989: 424). Tragically, despite his hope, the darkness overwhelmed him on the 5th of March 1944 when after shaving and washing near the officer's latrines, he was found dead with a single shot to the head, and his revolver in his hand. Despite the obvious suicide, the Board of Enquiry found charitably that he had tripped and accidentally shot himself.

Masculinity in its many facets in the Far East campaign was better illuminated by soldiers' letters and post-war memoirs than could be expressed in the *Calling Blighty* films. But there were also a very small number of filmed messages from women, mostly filmed in India. It might be imagined that the women's mode of expression would differ significantly from the men, but the five filmed messages that still exist (out of around 1200 in total) show a remarkably similar pattern. Relatively few women from the United Kingdom served in the Far East and most were nurses of the FANY (First Aid Nursing Yeomanry), Women's Air Force WAAF's, or served in the Women's Auxiliary Service (Burma), which ran mobile canteens for the Allied troops involved in the campaign. The Wasbies, as they were known, ran char wagons and canteens deep into Burma and sometimes within sound of the Japanese guns. They lived in dangerous and uncomfortable conditions and often improvised stoves from old ammunition boxes, and despite being evacuated from Myitkyina and Imphal, were flown back into the war zones as soon as the Japanese retreated. There were also the female servicewomen of the Women's Auxiliary Corps, formed in 1942, where British and Indian women could join on equal terms, and work in anti-aircraft direction finding and plotting, parachute inspection and ciphers as well as more traditional catering roles (Khan 2015: 154).

All the women who feature in the surviving films send greetings from Bombay or Ceylon, rather than Burma, but may have been flown there, as well of course had been many groups of men. More women than appear in the remaining films are mentioned in contemporary local newspaper reports, but there is no reason to believe the ratio of men to women, about 250 to 1, was any different in the films that have been lost. Molly Budgen was filmed on Malabar Hill, Bombay in the last ever *Calling Blighty* film produced, number 391, and speaks to her parents, and probably her sweetheart, 'Fred darling'. She spends most of her message dwelling on the mail situation. 'I hope my mail is getting through OK now. I think there was a hold up a while ago but it should be all right again. Yours is coming through fine and thanks a million for it all. I never had so much is I had lately'. As with many of the men the unfamiliar situation leads her to dry up. 'Well I seem to have forgotten everything I had to say so cheerio' [salutes] (*CB* 391 1946). Margaret Taylor, a member of the WRNS from Manchester, is also apprehensive, as she is introduced by a fellow sailor: 'Oh by the way we have a very nervous person behind the wall here'. In a cultured middle class accent she delivers her message to 'Mummy and Sheila'. 'I do hope you're all well. I'm fine. I'm going off on leave in a few days' time up country' (*CB* 178 1945). She was filmed at the Portuguese Bastion, the remains of the old colonial fort outside Colombo, Ceylon, where one of the surviving *Calling Blighty* servicemen Frank Risby was also filmed. We know from his account that that his ship stopped there for a brief time en route to somewhere else and that they played no part in the Far East campaign.

Betty Hedge, also a wren from Oldham, was filmed in the NAAFI studio set in Bombay. She hints tantalizingly 'I guess this is a surprise for you. Who knows I may be giving you a bigger surprise soon. A good one too'. The surprise was not that she was expecting but that she would be hopefully returning home in the near future. Betty shows a missing front tooth, which was far from unusual judging by the standards of dentistry displayed also by the men in the films (*CB* 52 1944). Myra Vingle delivers her message from the familiar Malabar Hill, in issue 385, which must have been one of the last editions produced in 1946. She speaks to her grandmother Mrs. Watts back in Bournemouth, part of a surprising number of personnel who address messages not to their parents but to an aunt or grandparents, hinting at fractured family relationships or death in the family. She was 'due to go home March 1st. Hope to spend leave in Kashmir. I will miss India very much' (*CB* 385 1946). Peacetime India, with the hot weather, the warm sea

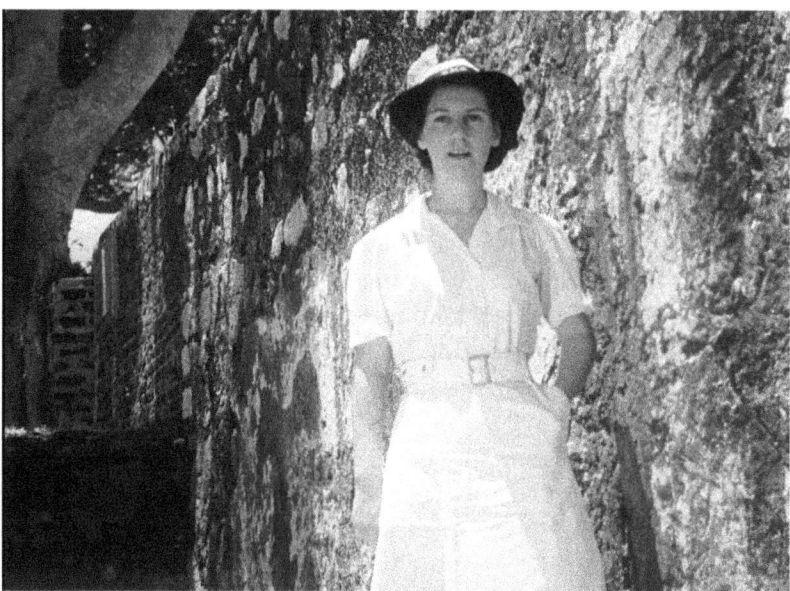

FIGURE 5.4: Margaret Taylor at the Portugese bastion Colombo (*CB* 178 1945). © IWM.

and the abundant tropical fruits of Bombay must have seemed a luxurious posting compared to the ration books and grimness of post-war England.

There is also an indication that some women in India were there with their husbands, presumably officers in the 14th Army. Pat Ramsden (her maiden name) sends greetings to her mother in Sheffield evidently from Malabar, as some of the other shots in the same film show men stuck on the beach in their lorry. In a distinctive upper middle class accent, she reassured her relatives 'Now you're not to worry about me because I shall be home before you can say Jack Robinson. Chris and I are both grateful for the lovely letters you keep sending us!' (*CB* 387 1946). Her identity and that of Chris (her husband?) have not been established, but the final shot is an unusual one, as the camera looks down over her shoulder high up on a balcony, symbolizing her authority, as a group of soldiers below wave good-bye to her and to Sheffield. Despite minor differences, the women in the films are treated exactly the same as the men, and their spoken preoccupations are the same.

In *Authoring the Self, Media, Voice and Testimony in Soldiers' Memoirs*, Lilie Chouliaraki (2016: 60) concludes that the western soldier's self-representation has shifted since World War I when the battlefield was observed as a strange place and the soldier as an 'other' within it. However, the *Calling Blighty* films do still reinforce the notion in the second war of Burma and the soldier's place there as the 'other'. There is little or no commentary on the country and almost nothing on the Burmese or Indian people themselves, apart from some asides about local landmarks, a pagoda or the opulent surroundings of a temple. Chouliaraki's formulation of a more recent practice of these soldiers considering, for example, the Iraqi or Afghani local as someone who 'shares a western sense of humanity' (2016: 60) is absent from the World War II films. Myra Vingle said that she would miss India very much, but there is little or nothing from the men that suggest they would miss Burma, or that they had much connection with it. Dick Fiddament was a private who served with the 2nd Bn Royal Norfolk Regt in Burma, 1940–45 and appears in the *Calling Blighty* film on the Irrawaddy river outside Mandalay. He reflected much later on his feeling of alienation from the country. 'In France although they speak a different language, there are brick buildings, it's like being with your own people so to speak. The Indians and the Burmese, parts of the British Empire; they didn't want us. They had no more thoughts of allegiance with us than the Japanese. On top of this you had malaria, dengue fever, prickly heat, jungle sores, dysentery. This is why you got despondent there' (Fiddament 1997: n.pag).

Ultimately the filmed messages and the powerful confrontation with the faces of the men and women on screen in the darkened atmosphere of the cinema are as significant for what is not said as much as what is uttered. The expressions of concern about the lack of mail or conventional requests to be remembered to an aunt or neighbour, elide positive silences and the silences continued post-war. Relatives at the screenings almost invariably said that their fathers or grandfathers never talked about their experiences, that their response to the events they had undergone remained unspoken. Jay Winter in *War Beyond Words* contends that the silences these men and women brought back from war were 'performative non-speech acts' exemplified by the two-minute silence on Armistice Day (Winter 2017: 173). These acts, the silences, have many different meanings. After the second war, there was a sense of looking forward to a newer, brighter future, not dwelling on the past, on painful memories; perhaps that servicemen felt that apart from their comrades, no one was really interested, or even understood, an experience that was unimaginable on the home front. There are also family silences, as Winter says that are 'kept by fathers and mothers, sisters and brothers, to enable ordinary life to go on after difficult events'. Many men experienced profound difficulties from the traumas they had undergone. Dick Fiddament resumed his home life as a butcher but was one of many men who fell into drinking and depression and was prescribed tranquilizers when he integrated back into the life he had left behind (Fiddament 1997: n.pag). Conventional notions of masculinity and stoicism were tested and found difficult to assimilate with the realities of a terrible conflict, unthinkable memories. This theme of silence and how it connects with remembrance I will develop in a later chapter; however the film screenings themselves were anything but silent.

6

The Invisible Men:
Empire Soldiers and *Calling Blighty*

Britain did not fight the Second World War, the Empire did.

(Khan 2015: xiii)

Tom Carew joked that SEAC stood for Saving England's Asian Colonies, and it is true that at its heart for Britain at least, the Far East campaign was a war waged by its colonies from around the world. Of the 690,000 men in the 14th army, only around 80,000 were British troops, the vast majority being from the Commonwealth. These were predominantly Indian but also East and West Africans (a surprisingly large number), Nepalese Gurkhas, Burmese, Karen and many other nationalities, even a West Indian Brigade. In terms of casualties, 14,000 fell in battle, of whom fewer than 5000 were Britons, the majority being from the colonies. Many more died of disease – the Commonwealth Force had over 73,000 who died or were wounded in total (compared to 200,000 Japanese) (McLynn 2011: 1). And yet the overwhelming impression gained from the *Calling Blighty* films in relation to the hundreds of thousands of Empire troops that the British troops fought alongside in some of the most arduous conditions of the war is one of invisibility. The men are literally relegated to the background, as servants, lifeguards, cameramen or as exotic extras in an Asian scene. Nor do they have a voice in the films; mute and inconspicuous or unseen, they are unable to utter anything, which can be compared with the many hours of speaking by the men and women from the United Kingdom. But there are still signs in the films that we can use to unravel the complex relationship between the wartime soldiers and the predominant attitudes to foreigners, Empire and the East itself.

Of course, the *Blighty* films were by definition 'spoken postcards' home to families in the United Kingdom; there was no reason why in this series the Commonwealth troops should be filmed delivering messages to their own families in Africa or India, or the Caribbean; if any such messages were filmed, they have not survived. Nor were films made of the 12,000 United States servicemen (McLynn 2011: 1) or the more numerous Chinese who also fought in what was in essence a parallel war to open up the Burma Road to China in order to bolster Chiang Kai-Shek's resistance to the Japanese there. The BBC did broadcast radio programmes such as *Calling All Canadians*, 'News from Canada and of Canadians on the fighting front, including a newsletter in French for French-speaking Canadians'. There was also a similar *Calling All Australians* feature and even for a brief time a radio programme *For the India Forces*, which was aimed at Indian troops who were serving in Britain and included recorded personal audio messages to be broadcast to families in India by courtesy of all India radio. This program presented by Damyant Sahni also included nostalgic Indian music and plays for the troops far from home (BBC Genome 2020: n.pag.). In fact the *Blighty* films had been allocated to the CKS, the Combined Kinematograph Services to produce when they were already creating educational films in Bombay for the Indian Army, films such as *Camouflage in the Field* (with commentary in Urdu, English and Gurkhali), but hardly any trace of this prior role remains in the surviving *Calling Blighty* films, which are all of British servicemen and women (Beckett 1992). Len England noted for Mass Observation, the social research organisation, in 1940 that support for the Indian troops, as gauged from audience reaction to their appearance in newsreels, was very strong, and that applause was noted when 'Dominion troops (particularly the Indians)' were on screen and that the longest was for a brief shot of Indian troops (England 2002: 189).

Why did the Commonwealth troops join up in such large numbers to fight a war on behalf of their colonizers? In India's case, the impetus is more understandable, as the Japanese overran Burma and were massing on the country's western border, but the motivations for the Gurkhas seem more unclear, and even less so for the thousands of East and West Africans who were shipped to India to fight for the British. In World War I, the numbers serving in the Indian army were even greater; 1.5 million in all, of whom over a million were sent overseas. Author of the book *India, Empire and First World War Culture*, Santanu Das notes India's 'phenomenal war enthusiasm', which perhaps overshadowed even the limited financial attractions of serving in the army (Das 2020: n.pag.). By the start of World War II, there were a number of reasons why Empire troops, willingly or unwillingly, were moved to join up and lay down their lives for the Empire. One was that many of the Princes who effectively ruled a third of the subcontinent, but who depended on British rule for their power and wealth, offered their direct military help to the Crown. They could afford to do so; the Nizam of Hyderabad had been featured on the front cover of *Time Magazine* in 1938, feted as the richest man in the world. The British Viceroy at the outbreak of war, Lord Linlithgow, a man with little passion for India and a rigid nineteenth century view of the social order of Empire, made little attempt to convince the vast body of Indians to fight in what seemed to him to be an obvious moral imperative (both his twin sons were fighting in Europe). Instead he prevaricated and met with the Princes and old friends of the Empire (page 7). And one by one, they promised support; the Maharaja of Kashmir offered two infantry battalions and a mountain battery as well as his own pledge to leave for any theatre of war. The Nizam set aside over £100,000 for the air Ministry, and the Maharaja of Jaipur was soon in North Africa inspecting his troops (Khan 2015: 7).

Still the Indian army was a volunteer army, not one of conscription. By late 1940, 20,000 men a month were joining up and by the end of the war, the army was over two million strong (Khan 2015: 18). There was a tradition of military service, particularly in the Northern states, and family expectations played a part. Many Jats, Rajputs, Sikhs and Pathans from the North joined up, and Punjabis made up 60 per cent of the army at the start of the war. Local landlords in the Punjab would act as recruiters in exchange for a lack of interference in their operations by the governor and the authorities (Khan 2015: 12). For other ethnic groups, the military was a traditional avenue for employment and financial support for their families, particularly the Sikhs. Information about the war and its aims was difficult to come by, and the new recruits' expectations were unclear. Many felt that India stood far from the sphere of any potential conflict. As the war progressed, the willing volunteers were supplemented by those who had their arms twisted by recruitment agents and landowners, and malnutrition was also a factor; service in the military meant food for oneself but also the ability to support a network of dependents.

In Nepal, there had been a tradition since the eighteenth century of migration to find military work in the south; the local word for Gurkha, lahure, indicates its roots in one who travels to Lahore to serve in the army (Khan 2015: 30). The Gurkhas were regarded rightly by the British as being tough, disciplined fighters, and despite some difficulties for recruiters due to the mountainous terrain, there was fertile ground for recruitment to the army, aided by financial incentives and gentle persuasion. The mountain kingdom had abolished slavery only fifteen years before the outbreak of war, and in what had recently been a feudal structure, there were many pressures for headmen and landlords to supply men and demonstrate their loyalty to the regime. This was often resisted by wives and mothers, knowing the sadness, the *dukkha*, that the enforced absence of their sons and husbands for many years and sometimes forever would cause to themselves and their families (Khan 2015: 32). But whilst they may have had little information as to the nature of the war, or the unforeseen invasion of Burma by the Japanese, the Indian and Gurkha troops would have been at least fighting on the borders of India and to some extent defending the subcontinent from invasion. No such motivation existed for the East and West African troops, who came from countries relatively untouched by the war to fight for the seat of an Empire 10,000 miles away, in an alien and highly unfamiliar continent.

In Burma, the names of African regiments became commonplace; the 82nd West African Division (the Nigerian and Gold Coast Brigades), the East African 22nd Brigade, the 81st West African Division and the Third Nigerian Brigade. These were troops from Nigeria, Sierra Leone, the Gambia and other countries including present-day Ghana, half a world away from the conflict. The men joined up because it was employment; the army provided a uniform, a living wage and food. The reasons for even the existence of the war were in most cases scarcely understood. The TV personality Griff Rhys Jones made a programme about his father's service in the Gold Coast Regiment, part of the 82nd Division, where he was a medical officer, one of 26 Europeans in a battalion of 1200 African men. In the programme, Burma, *My Father and the Forgotten Army* (2017), he interviewed Kofi Nortai, a medical orderly who had joined up and served with his father Elwyn. 'I was seventeen, eighteen years old. During that time, I knew nothing about the war. I heard drumming – they were marching. They said anybody who wants to join the army, they should come. Daybreak I go myself. I don't tell my mother or father'. The West Africans were valued by the British army for their willingness to follow orders and tradition of head carrying, useful to transport supplies in the jungle, despite the fact that the Africans had all been brought up on the grassland. Their tribal allegiance to the chief transferred partly to the completely white British officers who led them.

The African soldiers feature in one of the remaining *Calling Blighty* films, and there are frequent appearances by Indians and even Burmese, but they mostly hover in the margins of the films, figuratively and literally. The British men, focused on a home audience, seem very much located in their local towns or cities, standing apart from their tropical surroundings, but there are some telling linguistic and other connections with Burma and India. Many Indians appear in the constructed studio set in the Shree Studios Bombay, which as a fictional NAAFI canteen needed servants and charwallahs to lend authenticity to the scene. They move through the tables in the background, out of focus, in their white coats and turbans, all men, serving drinks and tea to the soldiers waiting to be called forward to speak. These blurred images are nearly the only representative pictures of Indians in the films, but they never come into focus, become sharp detailed images, instead hovering indistinctly behind the speaking servicemen or very occasionally coming to the foreground to put down a cup of tea.

Issue 199, filmed probably in late 1944, of men from Manchester and Stockport, is unique among the 60 remaining films, in that the subject is an African Brigade with British officers, and in addition the unknown director has seized the opportunity to also include portrayals of Indian civilians. The voice-over at the start of the film announces its 'Greetings Manchester from your boys of the 11th East Africa Division', then as an African soldier stripped to the waist

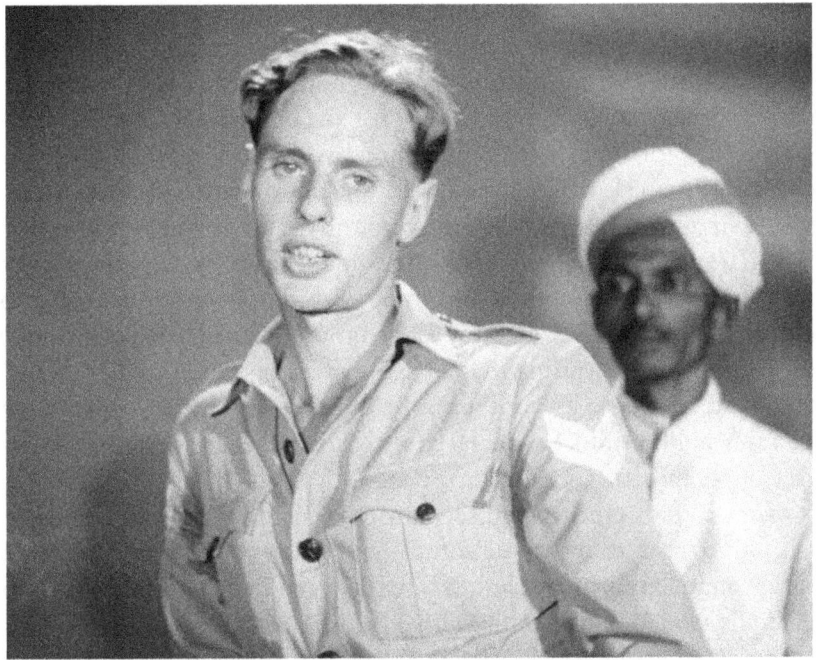

FIGURE 6.1: Indian servant in background at Shree studios (*CB* 99, 1944). © IWM.

is followed by a panning camera as he carries a log on his shoulders in an exaggerated leisurely manner, the voice continues 'from their victories in the Kabaw Valley' (*CB* 199 1945). This is also unusual in that the war is referred to; only Mandalay is similarly mentioned, and in that case men are filmed both outside and inside the ruined city just after it has been taken. The East African Division was formed in February 1943 primarily of troops from Kenya, Uganda, Nyasaland, Tanganyika, Northern Rhodesia and even the Belgian Congo. In the later part of 1944, after the siege of Kohima had been broken and the Japanese were being repulsed back down through Burma, the Division pursued them down the Kadaw Valley, the notorious 'Death Valley', so-called because of the high mortality rates from malaria (McLynn 2007: 37). From the Indian-Burmese border, the Division eventually reached and established bridgeheads over the Chindwin river and later some parts of the East African forces played a part in the successful battles of Meiktila and Mandalay.

The soldiers of the Division, the Askaris, were notable jungle fighters and were hardy and tenacious in battle both as combatants and as carriers and medical staff. There is a suggestion that some of the British officers considered them to have been undervalued and under used as frontline troops by the British commanders (Memorial Gates Campaigns Burma and India 2019: n.pag.). However, the opening scene of edition 199 shows none of this, and attempts to portray the opposite, in an obviously staged performance for the camera. As the African soldier reaches the centre of the frame, he is joined by a group of his fellow soldiers in the background who slowly put their own logs on the ground. From the right of the scene, a smaller British soldier runs in and starts to berate them in broken Swahili, apparently for their lack of effort, and he has to be restrained by another officer as the African soldiers start to argue with him in Swahili, saying they are tired and have been working all day. 'Eh, eh, Bombardier [speaks also in broken Swahili], your mother's waiting to hear'. The argumentative soldier then turns to the camera and speaks to his mother in Britain, mostly about his leave where he saw 'the Taj Mahal. I think you'll agree with me that there's plenty of nice places in India. Course this isn't one but [...]'.

This seems to be a constructed scenario in which the African troops are foregrounded, only to be portrayed in conformity with a 'lazy' stereotype, and then become again background extras in the shot, where they are directed to move their logs and other materials around in silence by another British officer. This must have been made with the participation of the East Africans themselves, under orders, but the dominant

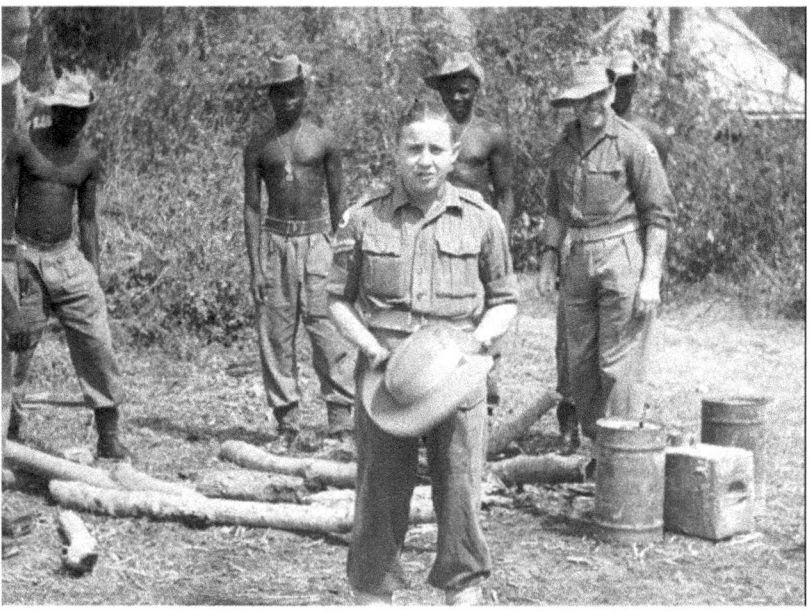

FIGURE 6.2: Manchester soldier and East African troops, Burma 1945 (*CB* 199). © IWM.

impression is less of a group of fighting comrades then a sharp division between an authoritarian white officer class and a subordinate black group of soldiers. However, at the end of this film, another staged scene seems to soften this image although still without referencing the soldiers' achievements in battle. After delivering his message, a Manchester soldier introduces the final scene: 'Now people of Manchester, having seen your relations in the East African forces you can now see the Africans relaxing in the evening. We're going to show you what we call an ingoma. We enjoy it very much when we see it'. At the edge of a forest, the Africans dance to an audience of British soldiers lined up in front of the trees. To the ecstatic sound of drum beats played by the men, and whistles, the African soldiers kneel down bare-chested, swaying exuberantly from side to side, their bodies decorated with white towels and plumes of extravagant grasses. They laugh and sing, and one man performs a somersault, and as they wind to a close the superimposed title comes up, The End.

The Ingoma is a dance known mostly in South Africa but derived from the name of the drum, or Ngoma used by Bantu nations and throughout the African Great Lakes region. It is thought it may have originated in Uganda, and ngoma ceremonies are used to assist in healing and social support and as a tool to unify the tribe (Wikipedia 2020). This final dance shows East Africans as the exotic other, an untamed and riotous entertainment for the white officers, but it at least steers away from the opening laziness trope. It is also possible that the voice-over, added later in the Bombay Studios, seeks to rebalance the constructed scenes almost certainly put together by the unknown director, with the voice's characterization of the Division as 'fresh from their victories'. The films are also rare in showing Indian civilians, but rather as 'colourful' dressing to the shots, as opposed to any real visual interest in their lives. So we see an Indian man hanging washing on a line, or rather pretending to, and two more sitting on a step watching the camera, somewhat incongruously as men tell of their homes in Moss Side or Stockport. In other shots, an Indian walks across carrying water buckets slung from a pole across his shoulders, and in a rare interaction, some Manchester soldiers play with an Indian child and hand him over to the next comrade as each comes to the front to speak.

The Manchester men all have the shoulder Insignia of the Division, a black rhinoceros head on a circular white background. Referred to as bombardiers, they are probably from the Divisional artillery the 302nd–304th East African field regiments. Whilst their roles are part of a structured and enacted performance, it is significant that the British officer speaks to the African troops in their shared second language. There are several points in the surviving films where British troops use Hindi phrases picked up over the years in India and Burma. In one film, for example, the Hindi phrase for OK is employed casually without apparent thought as to whether it would be understood at home: 'Glad you had your holiday with Dobs. From all accounts it seems to be Thik Hai' (*CB* 191 1945).

This phrase is used several times by men in different films, sometimes accompanied by a thumbs up sign. One man in Burma gestures at the spire of a pagoda behind him and exclaims 'Dekko!' (to look, in Hindi); another talks about chicos (children), and the family of a Brighton serviceman called Gibson may have been surprised when he said farewell to them using the Islamic greeting *Alaika Salaam*. Hindi, or a pidgin version of it was used widely in the Indian Army by British officers, and Field Marshal Slim was able to communicate directly with his troops in both Gurkhali and Hindi. He wrote before the war that 'The closest and the strongest link between officer and sepoy was their common language' (Khan 2015: 73). James Fenton was one of many British soldiers who had an interest in the Indians and Burmese, and he painted and sketched them many times, as well as trying to learn their languages. His paintings give a rounded view of the people of the countries he was in, as well as the landscape: character studies of Gurkhas, Hillmen in Assam, Sikhs and many others. He also took many photographs of civilians and especially children in India and Burma. 'Educating ourselves in Urdu has relapsed for a while. It was great fun testing our knowledge of the language on Indian tradesmen; chatting away like old women picking up more of the vocabulary.' However this was by no means shared by all his comrades, 'Many of the lads were unconcerned and had little sympathy or curiosity trying to talk to them or learn their language' (Fenton 2012: 142). Words such as *charwallah*, an Indian trader serving hot tea, *chico* (a child), *chota* (small), *dhobi* (laundryman) and other Hindi words freely pepper his letters home. Other Hindi words have become part of common usage in the United Kingdom, even to the present day. *Deolali*, for example, was an army camp in Maharashtra, from the middle of the nineteenth century. Soldiers frequently got camp fever or '*Deolali topa*' in Hindustani, which, shortened to the word '*doolally*', became a synonym for mental illness or general confusion.

A film made by the RAF film production unit in the first half of 1945, *Life in Command Southeast Asia*, apparently to encourage men bound for India, almost completely ignores the role of other nations in the campaign. Only in the Burmese segment are Indian and Burmese troops depicted and then only in the context of competing against the RAF in sporting events. For most of the film, as in the *Calling Blighty* films, the local people are depicted in background roles or as beggars – 'Some picturesque, all dirty, a few genuine'. They are characterized as subservient – 'You'll probably find plenty of Indian servants who work for you fairly cheaply', deceitful and lazy: 'Why bother, that's the Indian motto' (Osborne 2010: n.pag.).

Attitudes to the Empire troops and Indian civilians reflected a complex mixture of respect and disdain, depending on the individual and the context. The earliest Indian awards of the Victoria Cross in the war had come in February 1941 in North Africa, to Richpal Ram and Premindra Singh Bhagrat. While there was a sense that British and Indians fought 'shoulder to shoulder [...] acquiring a remarkable degree of admiration and friendship for each other' (as a British major later wrote, there was a difference between new officers recruited after the start of the war and older British officers who retained attitudes of empire from the 1930s. At the start of the war, treatment of Indians and Britons in the Indian Army differed – Indian officers could not sit on court-martials of British soldiers until 1943, and command of important operations was dominated by British commanders (Khan 2015: 71). Opinions also differed amongst commanders; Orde Wingate was 'known to have peculiar views about the racial composition of the Chindits, accepting Gurkhas and Burmese alongside the British, but no Indians on the grounds that they were second-rate troops' (McLynn 2012: 73). It was not until 2002 that a permanent memorial to the Empire forces was inaugurated in Britain, at the Memorial Gate on Constitution Hill in London celebrating the five million men and women from Africa, India and the Caribbean who served in both world wars. Since then, there has been much more stress by historians and TV programmes on the contribution of these forces, but VJ Day remains largely focused on the United Kingdom.

There were also by 1944 22,000 black US troops serving in India, and they suffered more overt racism, even from their own army. Black soldiers worked in segregated platoons and took on harder manual labour, including the extraordinarily arduous task of building the Ledo Road. There were segregated 'coloured' Red Cross canteens in Calcutta with black Red Cross women staff shipped in especially to serve in them (Khan 2015: 267). A black staff sergeant noted with anger in a military questionnaire that 'There are barber shops and hospitals at this base which will serve Chinese and Indians, but refuse to serve us' (Khan 2015: 270). The experience of the East and West African troops who served, nearly 100,000 of them, was possibly less oppressive, but in many practical ways, they were in a very different position to the British soldiers, not least because none of them were officers, who were practically exclusively white British. They were paid up to three times less than their white counterparts, and a lingering sense of injustice about this and the reduced war gratuity lump sum received at the end of service persists to the present day. A white private could earn ten shillings for each month of service, compared to three and a half shillings for a black African soldier of the same rank. Africans in the labour Corps got even less, about two shillings per month of service, but Asian personnel recruited in East Africa earned more than the black Africans but less than their white counterparts (Losh 2019: n.pag.). The inequity continued even after the war. Men of the 81st division from West Africa who had served bravely in the Arakan, returned to the Gold Coast to find unemployment and disappointment. When in February 1948 veterans of the war gathered at the Christianborg crossroads in Accra to protest, they were fired on, allegedly by the British commissioner of police, and three were shot dead. A decade later Ghana as it was renamed, became the first African colony to declare independence from the Empire.

There was at least one black British soldier, Benjamin Charles Macrae who has left his spoken memoirs, recorded by the Imperial War Museum, and who served in the 2nd Battalion Royal Norfolk Regiment. Although some men from this regiment were filmed on the outskirts of Mandalay by the *Calling Blighty* cameras, memorably introduced by their platoon commander Sam Horner, Macrae was not among them. 'Some of the men were. It was the luck of the draw actually. I never heard anything about it until it was practically done and gone. I didn't expect to' (McRae 1997: n.pag). He mentions casual racism experienced from his fellow soldiers, although not NCOs, but the worst experience was in 1942 in apartheid-era Cape Town, South Africa. He visits a Chinese restaurant with his friends from the regiment and was refused service. 'My mates said you serve him, or we walk out. I was quietly advised not to go there on my own'. His commander Sam Horner who was there describes the reaction of the fellow sergeants as 'violent' to the treatment of McRae; no discrimination is mentioned in India or Burma, a strong contrast to the experience of the much more numerous black American troops.

Two films that at least feature local people, albeit as 'interesting' local colour rather than in any meaningful way, can be seen by their stylistic similarities to very probably have been filmed by the same man, which is an indication that depictions of ethnic civilians were closely conditioned by the anonymous film directors. The surviving Birkenhead film and one of the Sheffield films produced towards the end of the war are both shot on Malabar beach in Bombay, they both begin with the same slow pan over the bay and they both end with men walking off waving goodbye over a similar wooden bridge on the beach. In the Birkenhead film, a man delivers his message standing next to an Indian girl of about seven or eight, holding an even smaller child. At the end, he gestures to her and says to his wife, 'Oh and May, by the way these two chicos don't belong to me you know. I haven't been here quite long enough' (*CB* 206 1945). The Sheffield film also features local Indians but in mute and rather incongruous supporting roles. In one scene, three Sheffield men walk up the beach, stop and deliver their spoken greetings one by one, whilst behind them an Indian lifeguard follows, stops and then walks off still shadowing them, all the time saying nothing. In the same film, a local civilian has as an interchange with a soldier where he actually speaks, if only to bargain in order to sell a pen to write home with – '10 chips (rupees)!'. This is the only sequence in any remaining film where an Indian is given a voice, even if the film shows that he is a street tradesman who is ultimately unsuccessful (the men address the camera to send their messages and so don't need the pen). In other scenes, three men

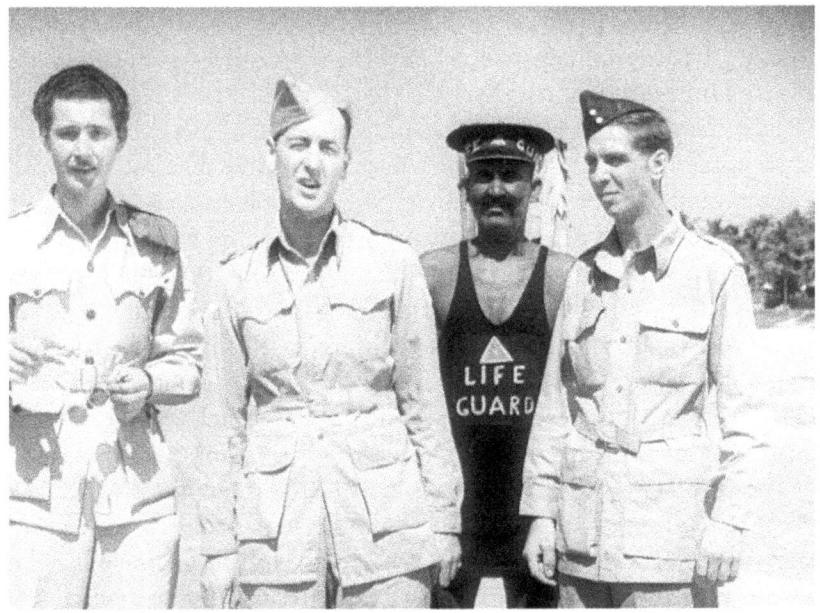

FIGURE 6.3: Indian Lifeguard and Sheffield soldiers, Malabar beach, Bombay (*CB* 206 1945).
© BFI.

on a different beach are introduced by a close-up of a small boy playing a drum
whilst two monkeys tethered by ropes to him 'dance' listlessly. The picture
of India one could glean from these fragments, however partial, is of subser-
vience, colourful poverty, especially of children, and a wiliness when dealing
financially with the British (*CB* 380 1946).

Not all Indians and Burmese were on the same side as the British. In India,
Subhas Chandra Bose (Netaji) was the leader of the Indian National Army,
the INA, who sided with the Japanese. The INA embraced a modern form of
nationalism and was committed to winning independence from the British, and
although relatively small, with around 43,000 foot-soldiers, it had a dispro-
portionate impact (Khan 2015: 118). The core constituted Indian soldiers
captured by the Japanese in Malaya and was facilitated by powerful stories of
discrimination based on racial privilege in the exodus from Burma after the
fall of Singapore. It was felt, with some truth, that the British had protected
their own welfare and secured escape routes for their own women and children first. The INA offered an inclusive vision of India without caste divisions
and recruited many women, especially into the famed Rani of Jhansi brigade;
however, the uneasy alliance with the Japanese proved difficult, and there were
doubts that the INA was in any sense a real partner of what was a competing

imperial power. In the event, only 8000 of Bose's troops saw action, against the British in the Imphal campaign in 1944, which led to their defeat and in many cases capture and death (Khan 2015: 208).

The Bengal famine of 1943 also led to anti-British sentiment. In all an estimated two to three million Bengalis died from a natural disaster that had multiple causes but was compounded by British administrative incompetence and a War Cabinet in London that blocked and delayed food imports that could have prevented further deaths. Bengal was at the time part of India and hence part of the British Empire, but even Wavell, the Viceroy of India after Linlithgow, accused the government of 'neglect, even sometimes hostility and contempt' (Khan 2015: 213). In Burma, the attitude of the different nationalities that made up the nation was even more polarized. Before the Japanese invasion in 1942, only tracks connected it to India and Siam, and the monsoon made the only road to China periodically impossible. The 17 million people spoke between them 126 languages (Khan 2015: 143). When Aung San, after two years of fighting the British decided to turn the Burma National Army against the Japanese in a nationwide rebellion, having seen the way the wind was blowing, Major Tom Carew was chosen to co-ordinate the uprising for the British. 'Yes I have loyalty to the Burmans', he remembered in 1978. 'Not to the British in Calcutta. We had to throw out the Japanese; after that they had to throw out the British. I saw no role for the British in Burma. The Burmans could run themselves' (Carew 2016: 191)

Little of this appears in the on-screen messages. The directors and cameramen who shot the *Blighty* films on location were aware that their main role was to get the men recorded in focus and with clear and undistorted sound. If the men's wellbeing could be accentuated by showing them in an idealized canteen or paddling in the sea in Bombay, then that was a bonus. But if they could depict some of the country to emphasize the exoticism of the location, either through the people or more often via landmarks and buildings, then this could signify, if not an actual holiday, then the strange attraction of the East. So a film might end, with a tilt up a religious pagoda (*CB* 203 1945), or in another, a man after delivering his speech says 'At the back of me here, you can see the Shwedagon pagoda, which I've told you about in my letters. I hope to be seeing it this week. Dekko!'. He turns around and gestures as the camera tilts upwards to show the richly decorated pagoda spire covered in gold leaf and framed by palm trees. The Shwedagon or Golden Dragon pagoda in Rangoon (Yangon) is the most celebrated shrine in Bombay, containing holy Buddhist relics. This film must have been made just after the British had retaken the city in May 1945 (*CB* 219 1945). Another film, which features Flying Officer Timmins with his ironic comments about Burma being a great place 'to die in', starts with a long pan following a Burmese man wearing a cotton lungyi striding into the camp where the men are seated; the title sequence also features a background of Burmese religious buildings (*CB* 210 1945).

Len Abbott, a film technician and sound recordist for the *Calling Blighty* films who had been in a mixed Indian/Gurkha/British unit before being seconded to the CKS, remembered the filming procedure. 'A group of fellows would be set up against a pagoda or some ornamental thing. A morning; there wasn't any rehearsal factor' (Abbott 1992). Camera operator Jack Atcheler was also aware that the main spotlight of these living letters had to be on the servicemen. 'One would come up to the bar; the camera would be behind the bar. The barman would be an Indian; the camera would pick him up and he would talk to the camera instead of the barman' (Atcheler 1991: n.pag).

There were some Indian personnel who were part of the *Blighty* film crews, one of the most celebrated being Narain Thapa who later became a filmmaker himself and wrote of his experiences in *The Boy from Lambata: Memoirs of a Combat Cameraman and Documentary-maker*. 'Though 70% of all the troops fighting on the Burma front were Indians, no one knew much about them because the British and American war correspondents gave publicity only to their nationals and ignored the Indian forces. In 1943–44 the Indian Army woke up to the need for training Indian servicemen and attaching them with the Indian formations, fighting in Burma'. He was trained as a combat cameraman at the 'Crank Handle College' in Calcutta despite his only previous experience being with a box Brownie, and three months later he was posted to Burma, his first assignments the *Calling Blighty* films. 'Though we were shooting the films away from the frontline, sound equipment often captured the effects of artillery shell bursts in the background. That helped us provide realistic background effects'. (Thapa 2004: 38–44). A photograph exists in the Imperial War Museum collection captioned 'The director Captain Hamilton-Webb (left) with the assistant cameraman Dennis Davis in Burma 1945'. The camera is described, but not the identity, or even the presence of the Indian cameraman behind the Akeley, who closely resembles Thapa.

The very last *Calling Blighty* film made, episode 391, of men and one woman from Brighton, has a curious coda, intended to provide a sign off not just to this film but the whole series. Shot for the most part on Malabar Hill Bombay in 1946, the last minute and a half of the film features a British director apparently in a studio and beside him an Indian cameraman operating the 35mm camera. 'Ready to shoot' he calls out. 'Yes sir'. 'Lights on, clapper'. Then as the clapper board is placed into shot, he is interrupted by a voice from behind the (second) camera filming him. 'Just a moment John. The *Calling Blightys* want you'. He reacts with feigned surprise. '*Calling Blighty*? What's *Calling Blighty* doing here? To photograph me? Well I'm afraid that I usually appear behind the camera not in front of it. However this is our last *Calling Blighty* and that being so, I really should

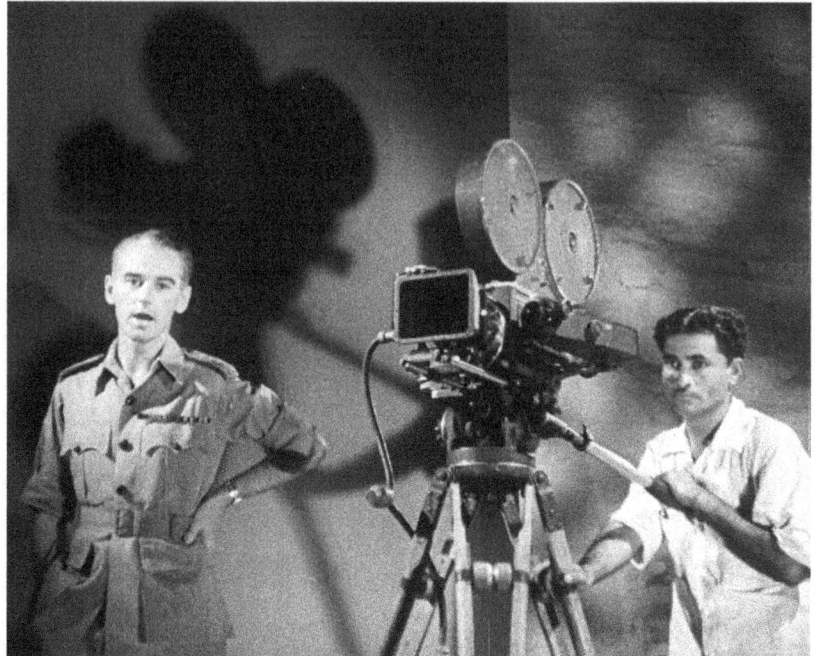

FIGURE 6.4: The very last *Calling Blighty* film made, issue 391. © IWM.

like to take this opportunity of thanking the camera crew and the personnel, who have given their utmost cooperation in making these productions the success they have been'. He then delivers a message to his wife and son Buster, while the Indian cameraman who is in shot the whole time, remains unnamed, invisible in plain sight (*CB* 391 1946).

7

'Dimmed by Happy Tears':
Remembrance, Ritual and Forgetting

*Commemoration is an active process, and often a contentious one.
When we memorialise the dead, we are sometimes desperate for
the truth, and sometimes for a comforting illusion. We remember
individually, out of grief and need. We remember as a society, with
a political agenda – we reach into the past for foundation myths of
our tribe, our nation.*

(Hilary Mantel, in *The Guardian* 2017)

Susan Howard's father Gordon Bowker, from Sheffield, was a Chindit with Orde
Wingate in a reconnaissance platoon, a young man of around 30 years old when he
was filmed for *Calling Blighty*. She knew the film existed because her mother and aunt
had spoken of seeing it during the war and checked on the website established by the
North West Film Archive with film clips of each man and their names where known.
'All of a sudden my dad came to the front. He wasn't introduced, he just said hi Anne
and hi Ada, hope to be looking after you and all that and I said God; it was just floods
of tears. He didn't say much about the war to be quite honest. I knew that he was with
Brigadier Wingate but I didn't know how tough it was. He didn't speak about it a
lot. He been there and done it and that was it, it was all behind him' (Howard 2017).

The *Blighty* films are just one site where groups and individuals can confront
notions of war and also notions of the family. These places are where groups and
individuals who were not in the war themselves can find in themselves a space
where their family memories become intermixed with public remembrance, sometimes uneasily. The entwining ideas that wrap around their, and our, reception
of these films are complex, mixing a nostalgic yearning for a vanished world, the
archetype of the heroic warrior, family memories and national communal remembrance. Why is it that despite the messages themselves being mostly so conventional, a ritual of greetings and orthodox phrases of hope, the films are so powerful

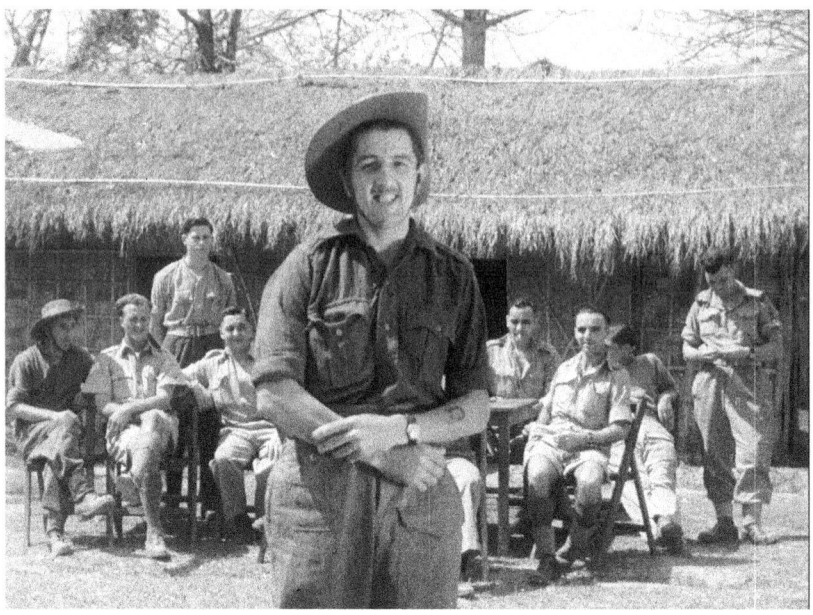

FIGURE 7.1: Susan Howard's father Gordon Bowker (*CB* 1945). © Yorkshire Film Archive.

for the families, both today and at the time? Here they are, back from the grave and not as we remember them in old age, but as young men, revisited as if in some time machine, messages from beyond, a profound and heightened confrontation with the living speaking departed. In many cases, although some wives are still alive, and grandchildren who remember and had strong relationships with the men as older grandparents, it is the father and son or father and daughter kinship that is evoked so intensely and stirs buried memories of childhood and the most crucial relationships of our lives. What was said might be stiff and guileless, but the effects are powerful; the silence of the departed replaced by its opposite, a tumultuous outpouring of personal and communal emotion.

The reception of the films mixed personal and public remembrance, on the vast canvas of a 'forgotten' mythic war of good against evil, where each of the men and women played some part. It raises all sorts of questions; how do we want to remember the men, as fathers and grandfathers, but also as courageous servicemen? As unsung warriors fighting for our present, their future? At one and the same time, these real men who we remember and we know were fallible, often scarred by a war they refused to talk about, are cast into a national need for mythic heroes. Nor were they all fighters; war needs the clerks, the trainers, the cooks, the tens of thousands of men who support the fighting troops. At such times, the causes of that particular sphere of world war, to reclaim a lost colony, with the collaboration of Empire troops, and Burma's rapid independence, are erased from the narrative, seemingly contradicting our present need for reassurance just as the audiences in 1944 also wanted their own consolation. The acts of remembrance arising from the films, which are both intensely personal and also focus on the drama of the theatre of war, illuminate what can be said and what cannot be said, and the contexts and rituals in which these different modes of remembering can be manifest. We have just, at the time of writing, completed a long period of a memorial of the centenary of the Great War, which has involved many millions of words, countless ceremonies and many artworks that seem to encapsulate, honour but also make meaning out of the carnage. One particular film that has emerged from these many tributes is Peter Jackson's 2018 documentary *They Shall Not Grow Old*, in which recorded testimony of men who served in the war is deftly edited with colourized film of the conflict to startlingly bring it to life for a contemporary audience. Jackson's film does not shy away from the realities of the men who served and survived, some of whom were deserters, many of whom were afraid and took their pleasures as men in war have done since war began, but he also respects the national narrative of the war to end wars, and audiences have warmly responded to his approach.

The contemporary wartime audience reactions to the *Calling Blighty* films are noted in newspaper reports and the memories of the relatives who were then children, for the most part, of the men who appeared in them and who were in the regional cinemas to see their fathers. The screenings were often crowded with families, parents and children, up to 700 at a single screening, and they could be repeated two or three times (Sargent 1992: 30). Often also they were shown as shorts before the main feature. These were highly charged events. 'Laughter and tears merged as mothers, wives, brothers, sisters, sweethearts and children saw 36 Bradford men who have been in India three and half years, who appeared before them one by one, talking, smiling, and betraying the emotion they tried to hide by some familiar mannerism of hands or head', the *Bradford News Chronicle* reported of a screening at the city's New Victoria cinema, (the 'first to be exhibited in the provinces') (*Bradford News Chronicle* 1944: 3). From the audience came exclamations of "there he is, there's Daddy" and "many wives" and mother's eyes were dimmed with happy tears' (*Telegraph and Argus* 1944: 3). There was humour but also ecstasy and physical and verbal expressions of emotion in inverse proportion to the subdued declarations on screen. In the Civic Hall, Exeter in June 1944 as the 'men stepped up to the microphone there were exclamations of recognition. "There's Daddy" cried one little girl' (*Western Morning News* 1944: 2). At the Regal, Oxford Road Manchester Michael Bolton of Miles Platting sitting on his mother's knee in July 1945 waved back to his father, LAC Albert Bolton speaking from Burma. It was noted there was an optimistic tone in all the messages ('it won't be long now') with some declaring they would be home for

Christmas (*Manchester Evening News* 1945: 2). Even in Ulster, where according to the *Larne Times*, the audiences were regarded as tough – 'While other audiences will applaud during or at the end of the film, those in Ulster just remain cold no matter how much they have enjoyed it. A little film dealing with Ulstermen serving abroad has broken the ice'. The crowds at the Imperial, Belfast, warmly cheered and on a more business-like note 'The cinema trade is hoping that many of these films will be available in the near future' (*Larne Times* 1944: 8).

This was often the first time in years that families got to see their husbands or sons in the flesh, as some had been on active service in the Far East for up to six years. From the very first London screening in 1943, where from the audience came 'clapping and happy cries, now here, now there, as soldier follows soldier in close up on the screen', pent up longing that had been suppressed could finally be released. At a screening at the Garrison Theatre in Liverpool in 1944, it was noted that some men 'took the matter very seriously, touched by the emotions of the moment, while others rattled off their simple homely messages of love with humour and gusto'. But whatever the message 'Many wives and mothers had wet eyes but smiling faces and the final applause was tremendous' (*Liverpool Daily Post* 1944: 3). It occurred to Marion Hewitt of the North West Film Archive and the author almost 75 years later, that these films, of which 23 are held by the Archive, had scarcely been seen since they were shown in regional cinemas to 'tears of joy' in wartime. We resolved to try and find the relatives of the men and recreate the screenings, discovering much to our surprise a communal but also highly personal experience that had the effect of a ritual or family service. The bitter-sweet feelings of the wartime audiences were mirrored in reactions from contemporary viewers, who often came with extended families, some who had been at the original screenings but also grandchildren and great-grandchildren. In November 2015, we held the first recreated screening of the Manchester *Blighty* films at HOME Manchester, where it was also filmed for a Channel 4 documentary, made by Oxford Scientific Films. This was followed by screenings in Sheffield, Birkenhead and Brighton.

Tracing the relatives was not easy. The Manchester films had been found in the town hall basement during renovations, 25 years previously, by an amazing stroke of good fortune, and even more so as the original call sheets were in the 35mm film canisters. These are the names and ranks of all the servicemen on the films, along with the home addresses of the relatives that had been invited to the screenings. Despite this, many of the addresses had disappeared due to clearances and rebuilding, most of the men and many relatives had died, and internet searches were largely fruitless. A few people had contacted the archive in previous decades, and their relatives had been identified, but to broaden this we created a website where every man in the films appeared as a short film clip with their names and a request to contact us and engaged

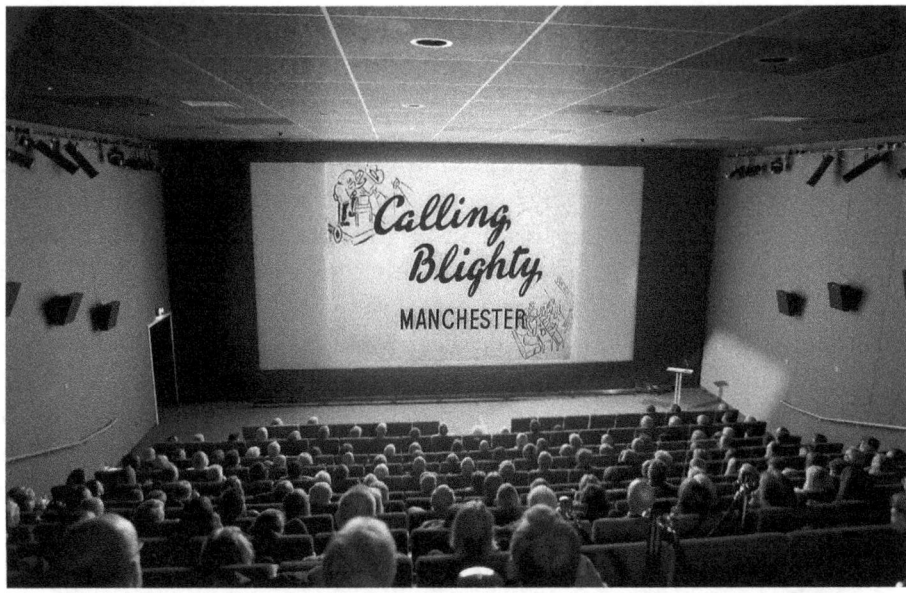

FIGURE 7.2: Manchester recreated *Calling Blighty* screening 2015. © North West Film Archive.

in a widespread media campaign on national radio and local TV, radio and press. Over a few months, we managed to identify 60 men and locate their relatives and invite them to the screening. This reimagining had coincidentally, as we found out, many of the elements of the original screenings. After a film to set the scene drawn from the resources of the archive, of the home front in Manchester in 1942, there was an edited compilation from the *Blighty* films showing the remarkable variety of responses, from humorous to deeply moving. We then showed a clip of each of the servicemen we had traced with a short identifying title, to a packed cinema of 250 relatives. There was also an address from a military expert, just as in the original showings: 'Major Griffiths, in a heartening little speech, stressed the value of regular letters from home' (*Liverpool Daily Post* 1944: 3).

We were also able to introduce two of the men still alive who appeared in the films to each other, Frank Risby and Ken Chadwick. This 'order of service' lasted about an hour, roughly the length of a mass, the individual soldiers were shown and honoured, and the reception afterwards also had faint religious echoes. The relatives from several generations that we had traced reacted with great warmth and emotion, even when they had already seen their ancestor's films, sometimes several times. Clearly, the ritual event was tapping into something that fused private and family memory and public remembrance. Ken Chadwick, interviewed in 2015 when he was 92 for the Channel 4 documentary, reflected on his filmed appearance. 'I'm afraid I didn't say a lot. In them days I don't think you are used to being filmed, or anything else like that'. And after the war, 'Once I got away from there that was it. I didn't think any more about it. It just came to an end'. 'Did you talk about it?' 'Not really, just got back to work and the lads you worked with, they had been to different places, and you just talked about it in general. There was nobody to speak to you about it really'. He served for four years from the age of 18 and felt 'I was very fortunate to go all through it because a lot of the casualties were from disease, malaria and other diseases. I was very fortunate' (Chadwick 2015).

Winsome March from Langley, Sheffield was a four-year-old child when she was taken to the Regent Cinema in Sheffield with her family. Her father had served in Burma since 1941 and she had never seen him. 'I didn't know what for, until I was sat there. I was actually stood on a chair because I was too small, and I remember this man coming on the screen, saying hello Winsome. I was shocked

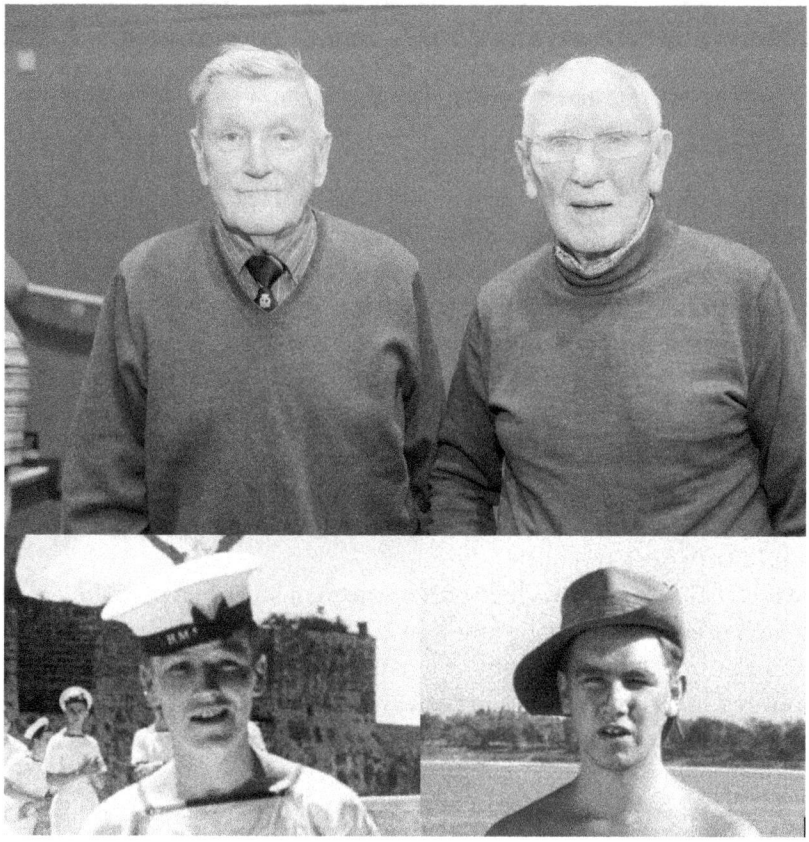

FIGURE 7.3: Frank Risby (left) and Ken Chadwick (right). © IWM and NWFA.

but excited at seeing my dad for the first time. I think a lot of people were crying and upset because I don't think many people knew what was happening over there'. She also attended the recreated screening at the Showroom cinema Sheffield in 2017. 'I think there were quite a few behind me that were tearful, me too. He was a tailor, and when he came back home he got a tailor's shop in Rotherham. He was a gentleman, and he didn't speak much about what had happened over there. He never actually told us what had happened'. Her father died at age 46 and maintained his silence about his wartime experiences (Rony Robinson 2017). Alan Parker recognized his father Wilf from his tattoo. 'He had got a tiger's head with a knife going through it, then there was a scroll on it. He had that inked in because he met my mum who was Margaret Palmer and he'd had another lady's name, and Mum demanded that he had that inked in'. When he saw the film in Sheffield many decades later, 'it was very emotional, I welled up a couple of times. I'm welling up now'. But his father's experience in wartime was completely unknown to him. 'You never talked about it, he never claimed his medals' (Rony Robinson 2017).

Jay Winter in *War Beyond Words* talks about these innumerable silences, mentioned again and again by relatives of the men who returned from India and Burma. There is a 'massive boundary separating what war does to human beings and what we can say about it' (Winter 2017: 173), and the silences that

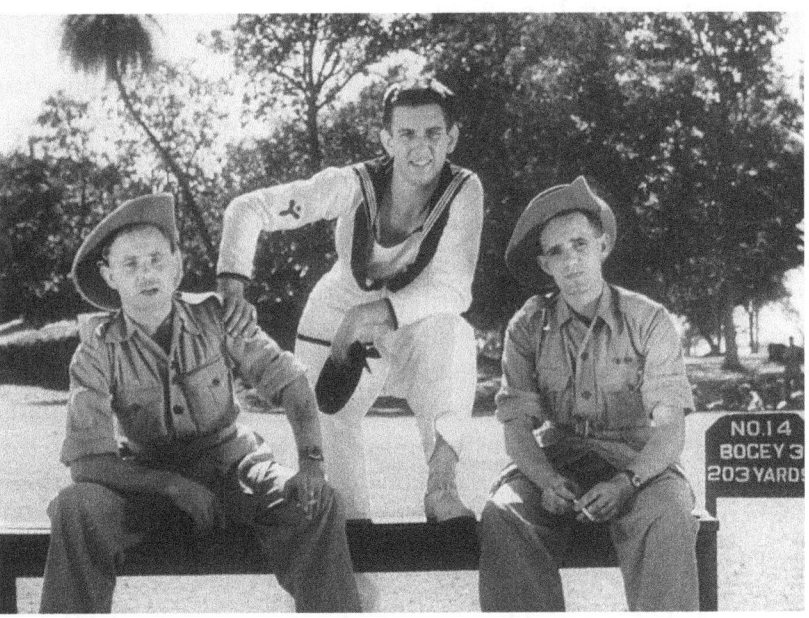

FIGURE 7.4: Wilf Parker (left) filmed on a golf course in Bombay, 1945 (*CB 252* 1946). © BFI.

men and women return with from the Far East have different meanings in different contexts. There is the two-minute silence at the Cenotaph every year, which connects with religious silences, a space for remembering and mourning, but also the silences of the perpetrators, enabled through guilt and a desire for forgetting. Why did the men say so little about the life-changing experience they had undergone? Ken Chadwick suggested that there was no one to talk to about it, and perhaps a sense that no-one would understand who had not been through the same events. The literary recluse J.D. Salinger opened up in his later life only to men that had served within the 4th Counter Intelligence Corps in the Battle of the Bulge and afterwards (Salerno 2013: 139). There was also a desire to forget trauma as a way of moving on from it, and the incompatibility of war memories with the daily nuts and bolts of family, and earning a living. There was a particular muteness about Burma, shown by the lack of cultural influence in present-day Britain of the country, especially compared to India, and the relative lack of a meaningful narrative that came out of the Far East war. The European theatre could be fitted into a story of success, of conquering the aggressor, but despite the Japanese defeat following the dropping of the atomic bomb, the story of Burma had no such neat conclusion. Harry Patch, the last surviving soldier of the Great War, only opened up to journalists about it aged 100, and even then said it was a miserable pointless part of his life; his mates had died for nothing. But silence, as Winter says is ultimately 'a language of remembrance'. It connotes meaning in itself (Winter 2017: 176).

The trauma of war also endured in ways that were also not easy to talk about, even if the desire had been there. Dick Fiddament remembered many years later in great and horrific detail his time in Burma: 'The vile smell, you never forget the smell of death', and after the war, he found it difficult to adapt. 'When I got home, I'd have these fits of depression, really really bad, and I'd relive it. Many a time I sat and unashamedly just wept. I couldn't control it. You were like brothers' (Fiddament 1997: n.pag). Susan Howard's father Gordon Bowker also suffered. 'I remember Mum saying he had terrible nightmares and things. Perhaps he just wanted to forget about it' (Rony Robinson 2017). But life had to go on. Rob Walker's grandfather was a miner from Rotherham who was called up despite being in a reserved occupation, as he was in the Territorial Army at the outbreak of war and served for five years. In his mid-30s, after postings in the United Kingdom, he served in the Yorks and Lancs Regiment in the Arakan and at the siege of Imphal where he was mentioned in dispatches and then harrying the Japanese back through Burma to Mandalay. He appeared in a *Calling Blighty* film made in a jungle clearing in Burma in 1944, introduced warmly as 'I'll now call on our friend good old Sergeant Major Stan Walker, God bless him'. He delivers his message in a strong South Yorkshire accent and then leads the men from Leeds,

Doncaster and Rotherham in a rendition of the Yorkshire anthem On Ilkla Moor Baht 'at (*CB* 1945). He returned one Thursday in 1945, and then on Friday, he went to the pit to get his old job back and the following day he secured a local allotment; on Monday, he started work and continued until he retired due to ill health, possibly caused by his experiences at Imphal. Rob had been searching for many years for the film, which he knew existed as his aunt remembers going to a cinema in York in wartime to see it. It was screened on Yorkshire TV as part of the North West Film Archive media appeal to find relatives ahead of the Sheffield

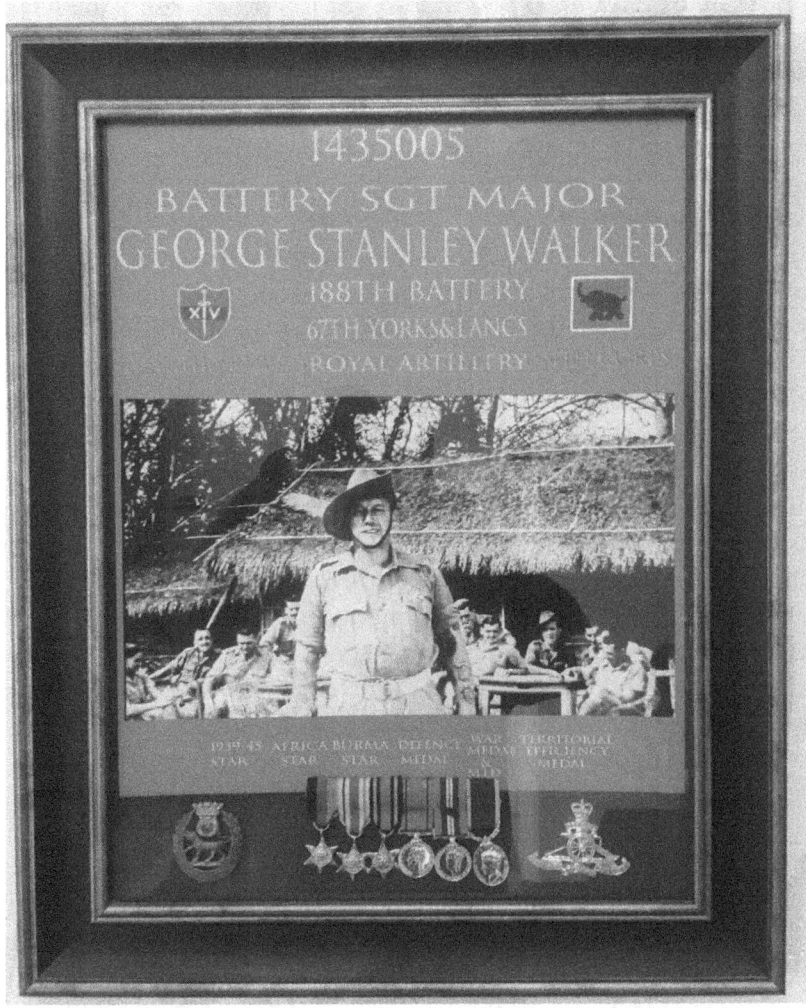

FIGURE 7.5: Sgt Major Stan Walker, created by his grandson. © Rob Walker.

screening, and Rob saw it. 'I said to my wife, I've just seen my granddad. She said it's not a ghost is it? if I had won the lottery it wouldn't have been as good as this' (Walker 2018: n.pag.).

The desire to memorialize a father or grandfather who had served in the war is powerful and enduring. Rob had researched Stan's service record over some years, through books and regimental diaries, and personal memories of those who knew him: 'One of his favourite songs was the Road to Mandalay, and when he worked at the pit with my Dad, another man would shout out to him, hey Stan do you remember when we were crossing the Irrawaddy?'. He has created a kind of shrine to his grandfather which hangs on his wall, with the photographs of Stan from the film, and emblems of the 14th army and IV corps, and images and descriptions of the medals he won (Walker 2018). He is not the only one to be so strongly motivated by a mixture of personal family remembrance combined with public memorial; Jay Winter has talked of a 'memory boom' in the latter part of the twentieth century (Winter 2006: 1). In an influential article, Alan Milward has said that 'affluence has helped to turn identity into a commodity to be consumed by everyone in leisure time' (Milward 2000: 8). The popularity of TV programmes such as *Who Do You Think You Are?* is based on (often celebrity) family history and the uncovering of secrets that link social histories to the personal, often with a strong outpouring of emotion. The various media representations of the *Calling Blighty* films fit into this genre, where 'history and memory are braided together in the public domain' (Winter 2006: 6).

As part of this process that mixes film with remembrance, the author also made at the request of the British Embassy in Myanmar, a film that was shown as part of the Remembrance Day 2016 commemoration in Rangoon. This film opens with images of the Taukkyan war cemetery in Rangoon, which contains over 6000 commonwealth burials from World War II, then showed film clips of soldiers who had later died in the war, delivering their messages in 1944, followed by close-ups of the inscriptions on their individual tombstones. The film was shown at a reception at the Ambassador's Residence on Remembrance Sunday to attendees from the British Legion, relatives of the fallen, and one living veteran of the war. Here the metaphorical connection between remembrance through a cemetery stone, and memorial through letters and films is made literal in the context of collective memory and war, a conjunction of graves and images like those found in some Eastern European cemeteries (Winter 2006: 109).

Foucault has viewed the archive either as 'monument', a historical artefact with a strong memory value, or the archive as 'document', an object to be critically questioned. In the latter sense, audio-visual archives, of which the *Calling Blighty* films are part, scattered through several different national film archives, play a role in mediating the past and can be re-used, re-edited and reinterpreted over time (Buchman and Mussou 2015: 1) both for mainstream media and other purposes including the recreated screenings. The reuse and reimagining of this material are given an added layer of complexity because of the status of the films also as artefacts of remembrance, their relationship to war and the servicemen depicted in them almost all of whom have died, some in action, but all of whom served. There are many, sometimes unwritten strictures on the use of archive film of war. The Imperial War Museum (IWM), for example, has a code of practice that excludes projects that are likely to 'to trivialize, sensationalize or demean the subject portrayed'. For sensitive material featuring footage of the dead or wounded amongst other types, they request a script of the project to 'ascertain its veracity'. For use in advertizing, the use of the material must not encourage misinterpretation, and colourization of black and white films as in Peter Jackson's *They Shall Not Grow Old* made in collaboration with the IWM is considered on a case-by-case basis (IWM 2019).

The *Calling Blighty* films have been reinterpreted in a number of different contexts, and it is to try and clarify these different modes of re-use that I classify them into three types, reflecting the three main outcomes from the whole project. These are *ritual ceremony* for communal screenings where the relatives of the men see the films in local cinemas as they were shown originally, *media memorial* for more popular broadcast media productions such as Peter Jackson's film, or the channel 4 documentary made about the *Blighty* project and *creative critical reflection*, reflecting Foucault's notion of the archive as an object to be critically questioned. In that category is the author's own film *War Memorial* that uses as source material the 30 surviving films from Manchester, Sheffield and York, and other experimental artists' approaches to war and remembrance, including films but also photographs, art installations and other artworks (Hawley 2019: 274). Choularaki suggests that both memories and military blogs are 'archival media that operate as states of memory' and reflect the 'soldiering self as a mnemonic force engaged in acts of remembrance' (Choularaki 2016: 61). The *Blighty* films are not reflective in this way, but their various filmic interpretations are. At heart, although unforeseen at the outset, the whole project examines how we commemorate, what can be said and what must remain silent and in what arena these different forms of memorial can operate.

In the ritual ceremony, the uncritical memorial is like an address in the church at the occasion of death; it is not the place for deep analysis, and it seeks to find positives in the deceased's life. The unexpressed codes of patriotism, heroism and sacrifice are not to be quizzed. The meaning of the war if it had any meaning is left unsaid although this is much clearer in the European front against Hitler than the colonial war against the Japanese in the Far East to defend the Empire, using a largely Empire army. The recreated cinema screenings had many elements of the original wartime film shows, for example, in the Bradford screening the families had been 'guests' of the Northern command welfare officer. In the HOME screening, we had a short talk by Col Glover from the Queen's Lancashire Regiment Museum. There was a closing filmed song of Lassie from Lancashire that the audience joined in with, and then a drinks reception where the families could share at length stories of their wartime relatives. Unknown to us at the time this closely resembled the wartime screenings; in the Bradford cinema in 1944, 'Afterwards over tea and sandwiches, officers who have seen Indian service described life at places where their men are serving' (*News Chronicle* 1944: n.pag.). The 'order of service' lasted roughly the length of a mass, the individual soldiers were shown and honoured as if communicants and the reception afterwards also had faint religious echoes. The relatives from several generations that we had traced reacted with great warmth and emotion, even when they had already seen their ancestor's films, sometimes several times. Clearly the ritual event was tapping into something that fused private and family memory and public remembrance.

It was also clear through anecdotal evidence that the straightforward process of reverential remembrance was sometimes clouded by complex family narratives. In one instance, we were told by the daughter of a man in the film that her brother who had been estranged from their late father had been able to reconcile his relationship with him by seeing the film, just before the brother himself had died. In another, not in Manchester, a son who had been traced through a wide radio and newspaper search seemed remarkably cool about seeing the film of his father, who he had called out to as a young child in 1944 according to a contemporary report when he had seen him in the cinema. He revealed that in fact he had been more or less abandoned by his lorry driver father and brought up by his grandparents. The healing process of reunion and memory did not always operate straightforwardly or at all.

The project also led to a popular *media memorial*, a TV programme that engaged with the contradictions of the war but focussed mainly on five personal narratives, a Channel 4 documentary produced by Oxford scientific films, *Messages Home, Lost Films of the British Army* (2016). The narrative trope of treasures lost and rediscovered, and secrets revealed were explored in the programme that, whilst historically accurate, was inevitably in the context of broadcast programming also highly geared to story-led television. The heroic warrior myth and the unexplored codes of patriotism and sacrifice were not confounded but in some ways reinforced. However, the broadcast did engage with collective remembrance in public recollection through these personal stories where the individual story stood for the whole conflict and gained wide and deserved popular acclaim. The media memorial does not set out to challenge accepted notions of remembrance,

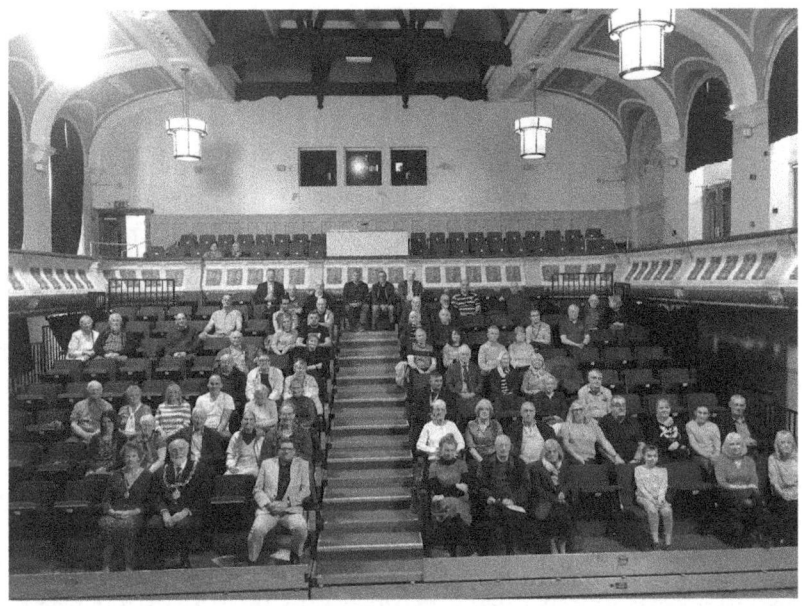

FIGURE 7.6: Birkenhead Town Hall at the screening of the films in 2018. © North West Film Archive.

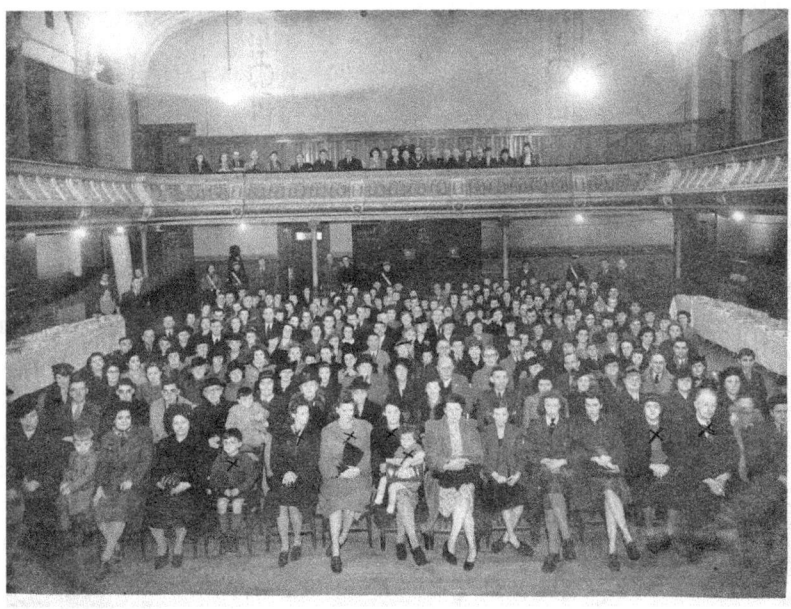

FIGURE 7.7: Birkenhead Town Hall at the original screening in 1946. © Joyce Whitley/ Ron Pinnington.

or to take a critical stance, the focus is mostly on uncovering secrets that are gradually revealed in the course of 50 minutes and is personality-led. The individual narrative stands for the whole, families are linked to heroism and stoicism, and there is often an emotional climax, loss and tears.

The program followed five individual men, one, Ken Chadwick, still alive, and their families, and through their stories tried to open up the narrative of the war in the Far East, and interweave family stories with military history. The stories were framed by military historian Rob Lyman and a voice-over by Paul McGann. There had been a suggestion of a female voice-over, perhaps Maxine Peake who had worked on a previous North West Film Archive production; however, the Channel 4 editor had apparently responded that the audience would not accept a woman within the context of military history, a response also noted by Jay Winter when Judi Dench was one of the voices on the major TV series 1914–18: *The Great War and the shaping of the Twentieth Century* (Winter 2006: 217). To give first-hand testimony of the terrible conditions in Burma, a living ex-Chindit veteran Harold Shippey talked powerfully about jungle warfare and the impact on the men of disease and death. This trope of the horrors of war was both real and naturally emphasized within a dramatic approach to the conflict but was not always the experience of the men involved. The author interviewed Dennis Porter, a Sheffield Burma veteran whose company had flushed the retreating Japanese out of villages in Burma in 1944 and who did not appear in the *Blighty* films, but his voice was included in a film made for a recreated Sheffield screening in order to set the context for local men who had been in the Fourteenth Army. He had only once fired his gun in anger, his only injuries came in training when his machine gun blew up on him, and of the long journeys across India in a cattle truck, he said 'I always enjoyed the travel'. However, the reality of disease and death was still very vivid to him (Porter 2016).

The television programme, part of the *Secret History* series, focused on revelation: Frank Miller's children thought he had served in the Catering Corps as a 'cabbage mechanic', but the emblem on his uniform showed he was a member of the 'legendary' Chindits. Frank Bramhall almost certainly suffered from PTSD for the rest of his life, undiagnosed and unremarked upon. One story of Anne Alsop took her to the Burma grave of her father John Hartley, who had died in action before she was born and who her mother after remarrying had erased from her life. When shown the film of her father for the first time in Manchester she showed relatively little emotion, but when asked to speak to her late father in front of his memorial stone in Rangoon, she became emotional and tearful, and the program overall emphasized loss and reconciliation. Another focused on Norman Ellor, whose sons had a rich cache of letters to and from his then sweetheart, who later became his wife, and these gave depth to the personal testimonial and allowed him to 'speak' from the past to reveal his hatred of war, at odds to his ebullient greeting on the film. Here the letters as read by his son could uncover the actuality of his experience, which was hidden behind the need for reassurance he projected on screen. One of two living veterans Ken Chadwick, then 92, was interviewed in the art deco Stockport Plaza Cinema, as he saw film of himself in 1944, but his response was remarkably free from trauma and bitterness. 'I look a bit fatter than I thought I was' was his chief reaction. The program was accurate in quietly revealing if not emphasizing the facts about the war in the Far East, that it was primarily to recapture colonies lost to the Japanese and that Indian soldiers had suffered the most casualties. However, one of the most telling sequences filmed of Lancashire men in Burma in 1944 showed just how many of the men delivering confident messages had been killed by the end of the war (*Messages Home* 2016).

The previous TV documentary *Burma, My Father and the Forgotten Army* (2013) in which comedian Griff Rhys Jones travelled to Ghana to trace his own father's history, as a doctor with a West African regiment, also operated as a media memorial, both as personal history and that of the Far East war, it was unusual in making explicit the way that African soldiers had been transported many thousands of miles to defend the Empire in wartime. Rhys Jones interviewed several African soldiers in their 90s and took one, Joshua Ennin of the 81st West African Division back to Burma. This was again personality, and indeed celebrity-led, but within the format managed to approach the causes of the Japanese campaign and the independence of Burma post-war, where it stated that the Labour government took the 'choice' to leave Burma early. It also looked at the post-war veterans march in the Gold Coast and linked this with the African colony's own independence to become Ghana.

Burma's Secret Jungle War with Joe Simpson (2016) was as the title suggests, another personality-led media memorial where the famous climber tried to retrace his father's steps in Burma/Myanmar, where his father Ian had served with the Chindits. They found themselves in a military emergency following democratic elections, and there were attempts to connect the contemporary situation with the war against the Japanese whilst recognizing the huge differences between the two. Of the huge reaction in the media to the Channel 4 programme on the *Calling Blighty* project, and the space it occupied 'between public remembrance and private memories' (Winter 2006: 206), the *Radio Times* perhaps came closest to identify the power of the *Blighty* films as filtered through the strictures of popular TV. 'The messages from a distant warzone, spoken directly to loved ones, are extraordinary to watch, partly because some have Hollywood-quality cinematography applied to ordinary lads stumbling through endearments ("I trust you are all well [...] I'm in the pink" and so on), and partly because the soldiers are so unfeasibly cheerful, given the fighting they were going through' (Butcher 2016: n.pag.).

The third category of media memorial was *creative critical reflection*, a critical and creative reinterpretation of the films, expressed in relation to the *Blighty* films through a 30-minute experimental film, *War Memorial* (2016), directed and edited by the author. Drawing on the difference between archive as monument, and the archive as document, an object to be critically questioned (Buchman and Mussou 2015: n.pag.), *War Memorial* treats the source *Blighty* films as document, to be critically examined, but also engages with and draws out their aesthetic and surreal qualities. The piece is not a didactic documentary but approaches, in intention at least, the quality of art. It examines notions of truth through creative approaches that do not pretend to documentary 'authenticity'. It shares some characteristics with other artists or filmmakers who have reworked archive footage to create new meanings such as the Austrian Martin Arnold, who takes small fragments of old films and re-edits them to create competitive musical structures, and in a more critical sense filmmakers such as Adam Curtis and Johan Grimonperez. Klaus Vom Bruch in *Das Propellerband* (1979) repeats a section of World War II film of German soldiers turning an aircraft propeller to examine notions of masculinity. More explicitly about remembrance, Chloe Dewe Matthew's photographs in the series *Shot At Dawn* (2014) depict the sites at which Allied World War I troops were executed for cowardice and desertion. Corner (in *The Art of Record* talks of three theoretical themes, one of which is arts or reportage (along with truth/viewpoints and institution/form), which maps onto this notion of creative reflection – 'The status of the documentary as aesthetic artefact and as referential record' in which one could reference the original *Calling Blighty* films (Corner 1996: 11).

The reasons for making *War Memorial* were the author's own practice as an artist/filmmaker, and partly because there were profound elements in the *Blighty* films that had remained unexplored in the context of television and family. This was a free and creative treatment of the images and sounds, rearranged in a way that was both as was hoped, respectful to the source material and what lay behind it, but also teased out some facets of the conflict and the men in a non-didactic way. This war was essentially a masculine narrative, but some women do appear in the *Calling Blighty* films, and this was a dimension that was brought out, along with references to death from the men themselves, and representation of the Commonwealth troops who formed the vast majority of the Fourteenth Army. One issue was as the *Radio Times* pointed out, the 'unfeasibly cheerful' demeanour of the men. Where two men were shown in a shot but only one was speaking, these were combined, so that the unspeaking halves of the image created long, almost still shots, where the two men appeared to be meditating or reflecting uncomfortably on their fate. This theme of introspection continues throughout the film, with individual men also cropped in the frame to exclude their companions, rare extended

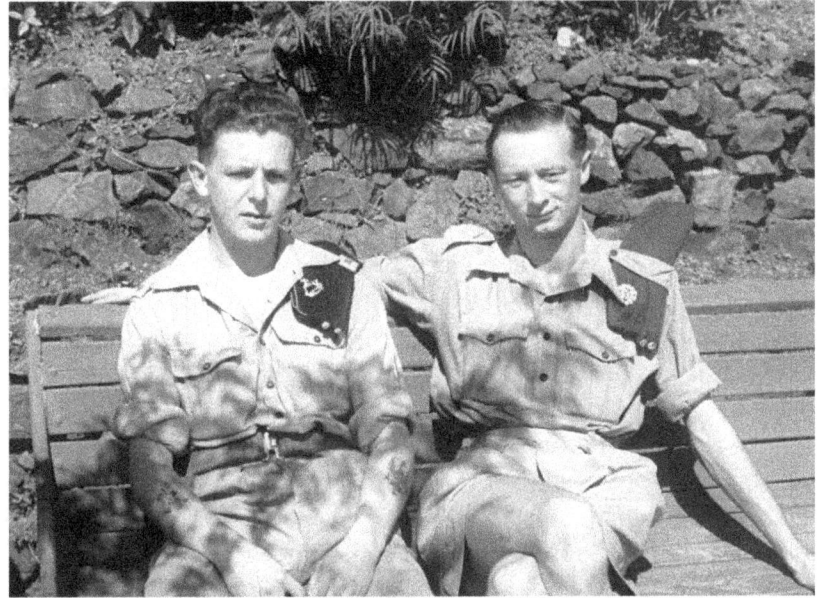

FIGURE 7.8: *War Memorial* 2016, combined image of soldiers in contemplation. © Steve Hawley.

shots of men from this era, not engaged in activity or speaking, but their faces reflecting their thoughts.

The ethics involved in the re-presentation of archive footage of all kinds, and particularly of men in wartime, is a complex and contested issue. The Imperial War Museum has its own rules; one example suggested that would not be allowed was the request by a production company making a music video for some generalized explosions. But there are occasions when a new context is being created for aesthetic reasons, and in any case, the complexities of a war such as the one in Burma makes almost every visual representation a partial and even partisan view. Changing attitudes and perspectives can also alter the ways in which film can be used. At a conference on archive film the author attended, a presenter representing an Archive stressed the way they would only allow their film to be used in a way that respected the context in which it had been shot, whilst behind him on a large screen originally silent film was playing with a jaunty and jarring 'twenties' soundtrack; the music altered the implied meaning of the film completely to a humorous and even trivial dimension. Music, voice and atmos tracks give richness to the aesthetic experience but present a determined point of view. TV producer Jerry Kuehl, who worked on the highly influential series *World at War* (1974), said of the TV documentary that it is 'not the doctoral dissertation, but the reflective essay in which nothing is said recklessly but in which the flow of the text is not burdened with a scholarly apparatus either' (Bryant 2015: 61).

The filmmaker Adam Curtis has developed his own style in which quotation and sampling, completely accepted in modern music, are used to devastating effect, in densely assembled films where a mixture of fictional (even *Carry On* films) and non-fiction sources are interwoven to deadly serious intent. There have also been many recent examples where a newly commissioned score has been played live over-edited archive film, for example, the English band British Sea Power's soundtrack for *From the Sea to the Land Beyond: Britain's Coast on Film* (2013). These creative interventions using archive could be loosely termed public history, creating ideas of the past from archives and other sources, and in sometimes oblique ways that are very different from those of an academic historian. Often in the popular media memorial, the same images appear and reappear, with different music and voice-over, such as the shot of Chindits in Burma trekking up a hill with their mules, which has figured in several recent TV representations of the war in Burma; in fact even the original film, a Pathé newsreel, *The Forgotten Army* from 1944 has music and voiceover that guides our interpretation of the images ('They look casual; it's the Japs who are worried'). In other cases, sober factual documentaries could prove unpalatable. John Huston's 1946 film *Let There Be Light,* made for the US Army, included the statement that 20 per cent of all American casualties in World War II were neurological or psychological in origin; the film was promptly banned and not screened until the 1981 Cannes Film Festival (Canby 1981: 6).

The Burma campaign and the Far East War are little represented in Britain itself in terms of substantial physical memorials. The National Memorial Arboretum in Staffordshire has sections for the Burma Railway Memorial and Burma Star Memorial, and there is the small Kohima museum in York, the only military museum exclusively covering the campaign. There are also a few plaques and stones throughout Britain, many placed by the Burma Star Association. The films represent an alternative and telling addition to the memorializing of this neglected conflict. They also reclaim the human face as central to the notion of the representation of war in the twentieth century. Winter has suggested that there has been a 'progressive occlusion of the human face and form', which mirrors the changing nature of warfare. He notes the way that the face of Anne Frank invariably illustrates the editions of her diaries, but Primo Levi, in his memoirs of the death camps, is never similarly represented on his book jackets (Winter 2017: 14). The faces of the men in the *Blighty* films, 8000 of them originally, stand as a testament in their humanity to the ordinary man in war.

The celebrated stone raised at Kohima has an inscription: 'When you go home, tell them of us and say, for your tomorrow we gave our today' (Allen 1984: xvii).

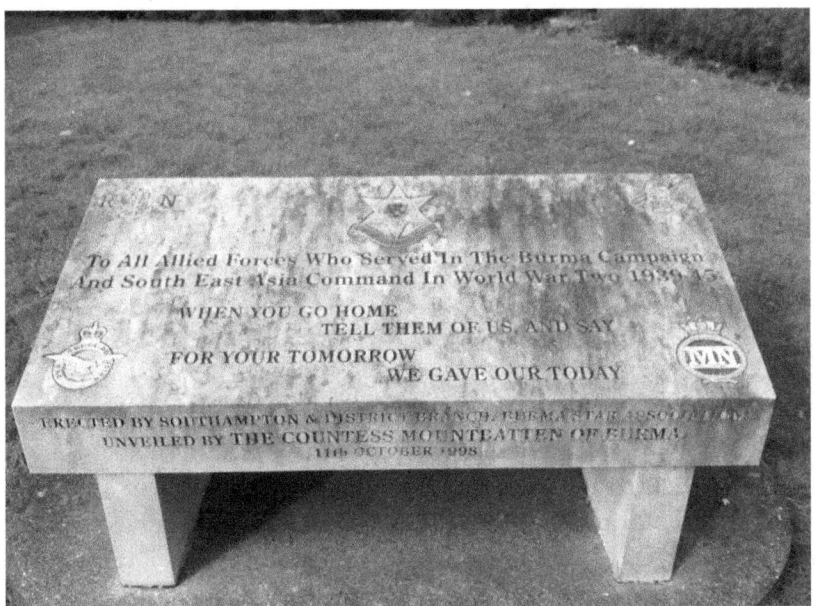

FIGURE 7.9: Commemoration bench in Southampton. © Steve Hawley.

The emphasis, as in much of remembrance, is on sacrifice, individual and collective. Individual sacrifice is of course still to be honoured; the giving of life to a common goal when required by a government or nation endures as the ultimate unselfish act by families and societies alike. But the notion of mass collective sacrifice, like older ideas of glory in war, is less certain. As Winter points out, the deaths of three-quarters of a million men in the Great War is a 'sacrifice' that would no longer be regarded as tolerable (Winter 2017: 114). There have also been suggestions that whilst we have been taught that the 'memorialising of collective historical memory has become one of humanity's highest moral obligations', that perhaps this is sometimes wrong. That perhaps to enable life to go on as it should, there is also 'an ethical imperative of forgetting' (Rieff 2016: n.pag.).

In *The cult of memory: When history does more harm than good*, David Rieff argues that historical memory as used by nations has often led to further war rather than peace (Rieff 2016: n.pag.). Remembrance can bring solace, binding a community or nation together in comforting solidarity, provided the nation was on the right side of course, but this eschews complex analysis for simple messages; sacrifice, glory and victory. Families can also cement their self-esteem with the consolation of an ancestor who served in a just cause. But the notion of what is just as not always clear-cut; the Japanese or German concepts of remembrance had to engage with this from the end of the war, as in the film *The Burmese Harp* [*Biruma no Tategoto*] (1956) where remembrance is also mingled with redemption. But even in the United Kingdom, common notions of an ethical war are inevitably clouded in some theatres, for example, Bomber Command in World War II, where the individual heroism and sacrifice of the airmen, half of whom died on operations, has conflicted with the inevitable and widespread deaths of German civilians because of the policy of area bombing. The memory boom still embraces World War I, despite all the participants now having passed away, but no one now celebrates the Second Anglo-Boer War, just a few years before World War I, where the British established the first concentration camps in which thousands of women and children died. Reiff suggests that states and political parties embrace collective historical memory to foster national unity, but that this can perpetuate and blight nations when allied with nationalist populism. Yugoslavia was riven in the 1990s with historical enmities going back on the Serbian side even to the Battle of Kosovo Polje in 1389, a defeat against the Turks that has a religious and nationalistic significance in the Serbian cultural memory seven centuries later.

Reiff does not advocate cultural amnesia; individuals must still be remembered and honoured, but life must proceed; even mourning must end at some point. It was in the edict of Nantes in 1598, that Henri IV forbade all subjects, both Protestants and Catholic, to remember all events that had taken place in the religious wars in France – 'The memory of all things [...] will remain extinguished and treated as something that did not take place'. The edict was eventually repealed and we cannot know whether it worked or not, but there are parallels with the silences that endured after the WWII in the Far East, silences that enable forgetting and enable damaged lives to continue (Rieff 2016: n.pag.). The *Calling Blighty* films stand as memorials to individuals, living breathing men and women, connecting them to now distant relatives, mothers, wives, sweethearts and children. They will gain more significance as the 75th anniversary of VJ Day gives way to the 100th. Simon Jenkins has suggested that 'memory distorts and emotionalises history. By its nature it dwells on grievance, emnity and retribution. Why is it we recall war but never peace?' (Jenkins 2019: n.pag.). As war recedes, the films will remain, and the portraits of the human faces restore memory to the personal, and the local, the typical turn of phrase, the pint in the local pub, the football team and the very presence of human qualities; of being alive and being there.

Conclusion

Time is the longest distance between two places.

(Tennessee Williams, *The Glass Menagerie* 1944)

It was at 38 Curzon Street in central London that the first *Calling Blighty* film was screened on 16th September 1943. The Curzon was the armed forces cinema in London, and there was an army officer managing it (Aldgate and Richards 1986: 110). There is a coincidental echo of British empirical power in its name, as it was the later George Nathaniel Curzon, totally dedicated to the idea of Empire, who was Viceroy of India from 1899 to 1906. The location of the Curzon cinema in Mayfair, the heart of Britain's power and wealth, seems symbolic of how the Far East colonies had been central to the spread of the British flag across the world. From this small beginning at the seat of the power of the Empire, the cinema screenings of the *Calling Blighty* films also reached out across the whole of the United Kingdom, extending into the towns and cities and regions of England, Wales, Scotland and Northern Ireland, as living portraits (however incomplete) of the men and a few women of the British Isles at a crucial time in the nation's history.

The films created a kind of census, a sample of men from across the country, seen speaking and looking directly into the camera, and seemingly at us, viewers across the generations. The immense range of British regional accents was represented, but also songs ('The Bonnie Banks o' Loch Lomond'), references to local newspapers ('I hope you'll send me the Mexborough and Swinton Times regularly'), football and rugby teams and local landmarks ('Tell him to get one or two rabbits on t'common') (*CB* 1945). This does not exist in any other culture at that time, and although 330 of the films have apparently been lost, it is not inconceivable that more will turn up. In 2017 a previously unknown nitrate film of Birkenhead men was found in the Wirral Archives, which formed the basis of a recreated screening in the town hall in 2018, the same venue that the original had taken place in 1945. Every film that was shipped to the United Kingdom was mirrored by a reference copy that was kept at Caltex house (since demolished) in Bombay, and it is not beyond hope that some of these may still exist.

123

This unintended survey of the working-class voice, uncensored if constrained by the army and family, preceded the explosion of working-class and especially northern voices into the British novel and films of the late 1950s by a good fifteen years. Even in the Free Cinema movement spearheaded by Lindsay Anderson and Tony Richardson amongst others from 1956, the working class appears as so much poetic material to be scrutinized from a distance. Karel Reisz in his 1959 film *We Are The Lambeth Boys* filmed young men and women from a London youth club speaking spontaneously, but their voices are 'explained' rather patronizingly by a middle-class voiceover. Free Cinema was also resolutely based in London, even if it did venture south of the river and to the East End. Joseph Janni, the Italian from Milan who produced *A Kind Of Loving* in 1962, said in comparing British to contemporary Italian cinema 'In those days England had forgotten she possessed provinces' (Walker 2005: 109). The men of the *Calling Blighty* films, most from the provinces, some the same age as the Lambeth boys but half a generation earlier, are restrained, even controlled by external and internal forces; the officer 'interviewing' them, the welfare officer behind the camera, the hierarchy and command structure of the army, but also their own struggle to imagine a presence on screen, the time constraints of the message format and the split between the reality of war and the home and family as they were addressing. Even on radio, it was standard practice in the BBC up until the mid 1950s for researchers to interview working-class subjects whose words would be rewritten by scriptwriters, to be re-voiced and recorded by the very same subjects, leading to stilted voices as non-actors had to act to present their own views (Young 2010: 147).

As masculine expression, some of the films conform to stereotypes of men in war, but not many. A few, especially the men from Worcester and Norfolk in Mandalay just after it was taken, show men determined and warlike, machine guns and rifles slung over their shoulders or a cigar clamped between their teeth. Len Abbott, a sound recordist said of the *Calling Blighty* men that they were a bit hard and often not long out of battle, caring little for discipline, but there is little evidence of that in the films, and there is a wide variety of different ways that the men found to project themselves. Sometimes the expression is tender, speaking of distant families and unseen children, or by turns cocky, intimidated and nervous, or jovial, talking of neighbours, beer, food and home. A key feeling that emerges in the films is how to sum up the nature of home, from a distant and alien land that was mostly unimaginable to their loved ones in the stalls of their local cinema. Thumim suggests understanding self-representation in three dimensions: institutional, textual and cultural (Thumim 2012: 166). The *Blighty* films have to be read in all these ways, the institutional processes, structures and debates shaping the films and what is said; the aesthetics, tone and narrative of the way they are filmed and the ideas, and the expectations, emotions and assumptions of audience or participants as they go to see them. Only then can the full richness of the films be decoded after the initial encounter with the messages from the past.

The *Calling Blighty* films are unique in World War II; they were both of the wartime fiction, propaganda and documentary output but also stand apart from it. They were (and are) documents but not documentaries, filmed messages that seem partly written postcards, half performances, sometimes banal (although not to the families, wives and sweethearts who viewed them) but often funny, or emotional or cripplingly hesitant or laconic. The message might often be formulaic, but the production values were of cinematic quality; 35mm films shot with superb sound in elaborate studios or on location, often with music in the background or to conclude. The reception of the films was also cinematic; they were shown in commercial regional cinemas, often very large ones like the 2500 seater Regent in Sheffield and in a heightened family atmosphere, partly an afternoon out, partly a secular service. The informal style of presentation that was unknown at the time only started to be taken up by television in the 1950s but has since become so accepted as to be the expectation.

The last films made were well into 1946, when almost a year after VJ Day the British Army still had a strong presence in the East, especially in Malaya. But by this time the frame of reference that prompted the long conflict, to protect a large empire, had altered. The tide of independence that war had held back had surged across the Far East and the Commonwealth was on the point of breaking up. Burma had been on its way to self-rule within the Empire since the mid-1930s but despite the bitter war to reoccupy the country it achieved full independence less than three years later, on the 4th of January 1948, the first British colony to exit the Commonwealth since America in 1776. How had this come to pass?

The government of Burma act of 1936 had allowed the country to have its own home rule, but within the Commonwealth and with the caveat that allowed the British governor to exercise all powers in an emergency. Ironically, it was the occupation by Japan that gave concrete hopes for full independence, as in August 1943 Burma was issued the status of independent state by the Japanese, with a joint Japanese-Burmese administration. The popular and charismatic Aung San was given the rank of major-general and appointed minister of defence and had originally fought against the British with his Burma National Army. Nationalist sentiment grew, accompanied by disillusionment with the Japanese, but post-war all the British could offer was a promise of self-rule within the Empire, which seemed to turn the clock back to 1939. Aung San emerged as the strongman of the country, prepared to call national strikes to intimidate the British, with a veiled threat of military action to back them up. Britain was weakened by WWII, and there was no mood to march back into Burma to engage in what could become a further long colonial war. The pro-Empire Burmese governor Dornand-Smith was replaced (he was said to be ill) with Mountbatten's ally Brigadier Hubert Rance, and simultaneously Indian Independence was on the horizon. In the high-stakes political poker game, Aung Sang held all the cards, the support of the people backed up by the threat of force; the United Kingdom was weak and Prime Minister Attlee who was a colonial expert with sympathies for Burma and India could not face another armed conflict. The British government capitulated and gave the Burmese the 'choice' of their remaining in the Commonwealth or not. In reality, there was no choice; Independence was the only option they desired (Tewson 2016: 16–30).

So despite Slim's brilliant military strategy and the 14th Army's achievements in pushing the Japanese back down through Burma, the ultimate aim failed. One of the few politicians who completely disagreed with this result was Churchill, who called it a 'dismal transaction' and foresaw 'savage slaughter'. He also continued to deride Aung San as a traitor who had his hands 'dyed with British and loyal Burmese blood'. Nor was the outcome a good one for the Burmese people. Aung San was himself assassinated in July 1947 by internal factions, leaving the country open to confusion and factionalism, leading to one of the world's longest civil wars, and a 50-year period of military rule that only ended in 2011 and at the time of writing has resumed. It is perhaps unlikely that the men in the *Calling Blighty* films gave much detailed thought to the fate of the country they had fought in, their strong desire being to forget and to get on with their lives and their families. The legacy of British rule has left almost no cultural echoes of Burma in the United Kingdom, and there is no simplistic positive narrative to sum up the war, apart from Slim's victory and sporadic tales of Chindit bravery and of course the individual heroism of the men who fought in the most inhospitable country and conditions.

The *Calling Blighty* films attract, as does a lodestone, conflicting notions of memory and remembrance. Whilst they are ephemeral and not traditional memorials in stone, nor performed national ceremonies of remembrance, they nonetheless have attributes of the memorial. The screening in Rangoon for Remembrance Day makes an overt link back to the memorial stone, connecting this through the moving image to the living, breathing soldiers who served and then fell in battle. As instruments of remembrance, they combine national narratives with family narratives, both in the three modes of secular service, media memorial and critical reflection, but also in terms of how they enable solace and reconciliation. Families reconnect through the recreated screenings with fathers and grandfathers (and one or two grandmothers) who nearly all remained silent about the war during their lifetimes and the screenings re-establishes their place in both personal and collective history. Sometimes for succeeding generations, this also becomes a healing ritual.

The films play a part in what Halbwachs calls collective memory, collective remembrance. This is different to passive memory, the personal recollections and introspection of a silent individual and rather gathers together fragments of the past and joins them together in the public sphere as a collective memory. This is 'socially framed'; it enters a domain beyond the personal individual memory. As time goes on, these collective memories weaken as the individuals who formed the group die out and the link with the present dissolves (Halbwachs 1980: 48). The Burma Star Association was wound up in April 2020 and its assets merged with the Burma Star Memorial fund. The association had been set up in the early 1950s when many tens of thousands of World War II veterans who had served in Burma and been awarded the Burma Star decoration were still alive and active. Seventy years later, only a handful remain alive; however in the *Blighty* films, a thousand or more men and women who appear in them will always be seen as they were in wartime, speaking smiling, connecting with home and wives and family and children. In truth in these films, 'They grow not old'.

The way we engage with the films depends on our relationship to them and the men in them although I would suggest it impossible not to feel a sense of awe and recognition of the human face of a wartime army. As popular media memorials, they engage with collective histories, leaving sacrifice in place but not disturbing notions of a just and triumphant war. Critical reworking of the films on the other hand can take apart the moving images and reassemble fragments for creative purposes to explore uncertainty and doubt. Above all, the personal experiences of family members seeing the films in cinemas just as their relations did two generations earlier are a profound encounter with the humanity of the past, unlocking intimate memories framed by history in an atmosphere of secular service.

Memory is also framed by technology, and the expanding technological means of preserving and extending memory from the start of the twentieth century onwards. Oral narratives can fade; knowledge of the Battle of Megiddo three-and-a-half millennia ago depends on the invention of writing, inscribed on the temple walls at Amun. The *Blighty* films were made possible by the innovation of recorded sound, synchronized with 35mm high-quality film, extended out from the film studio by the needs of newsreels but used for the first time as a living message format to improve the morale of a group of men fighting a distant war. The memory boom of the twentieth century has accelerated alongside further technological advances, first audio and video recording and now the internet. These have made it possible to capture and circulate images of war and the voices and faces of the victims of war as never before but crucially have linked archives of war and family on the internet to a generation eager to connect with the past. DNA testing has enabled a partial answer to the question, who am I and where do I come from, but expressed as percentages and probabilities, without a human face. Memory archives and museums have proliferated from the 1980s, but it is through the internet that an individual can find the tools via genealogical websites, such as Ancestry.com and Find My Past, to explore family trees, military records and answer the question perceptively posed by the popular TV series: *Who Do You Think You Are?* One man prophetically mused in a Birkenhead film that it was a pity this was not television, and 75 years later instantaneous video messages are now available through Skype and numerous other platforms. The *Calling Blighty* films were a precursor of both these innovations; like a one-way FaceTime call, they gave for the first time a visual and verbal message medium across the world, at the earliest limit of the preservation of family and collective memories in living breathing form. The aim of the North West Film Archive is to collect all the films in one place, as an audio-visual memorial website that future generations of relatives as well as historians can refer to, where family stories can be embedded in a wider historical context and create links between generations, especially grandparents and grandchildren.

The ultimate understanding of the films will perhaps emerge in the future. Only a decade ago, they were little known, for whilst they certainly existed in archives and through the writings especially of Paul Sargent, their reverberations within a wider consciousness had yet to be heard. They combine the mechanical with the affecting, stiffness with yearning, sincerity with matter of fact acceptance, and a deep quality of consolation. On screen for the first time, they speak to us from the distant past, proof that the dead can come back and talk with us. The *Calling Blighty* films shrink time, because of their cinematic quality, the direct address to camera of the men and women and their guileless self-presentation, often revealing deep feeling behind their wartime reserve. If war brings together personal family history and greater global history, then the *Blighty* films are balanced between these two poles, with profound significance for the relatives of the service personnel depicted, but also rich with meaning about the hidden war they were engaged in.

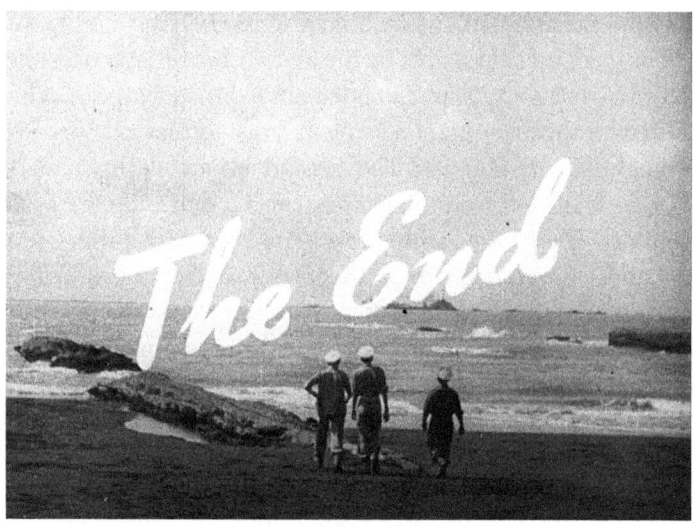

FIGURE C.1: *Calling Blighty* film 1945 final shot. © IWM.

Surviving Calling Blighty *films*

Issue	Location	Year	Film Archive/ catalogue reference
35	Dundee	1944	IWM 4058
41	Leicester	1944	MACE
50	Norwich	1944	EAFA 431
52	Oldham	1944	IWM 2221
56	Worcester	1944	IWM 3550
57	Dundee	1944	IWM 4059
58	St Helens	1944	IWM 2219
59	Warrington	1944	IWM 4161
82	Manchester	1944	IWM 3490
86	Sheffield	1944	BFI
85	Manchester	1944	IWM 3511
89	Brighton	1944	IWM 1449
99	Manchester	1944	IWM 3491
126	Sheffield	1944	BFI
132	Manchester	1945	IWM 3667
135	Sheffield	1945	BFI
149	Manchester	1945	IWM 3492
151	Brighton	1945	IWM 5063
155	Leicester	1945	MACE
164?	Manchester	1945	IWM 3493
178	Manchester	1945	IWM 3494
180	Brighton/Sussex	1945	IWM 5062
183	Manchester	1945	IWM 3495
186	Dundee	1945	IWM 4060

(*Continued*)

Issue	Location	Year	Film Archive/ catalogue reference
191	Manchester	1945	IWM 3496
199	Manchester	1945	IWM 3497
203	Manchester	1945	IWM 3498
205	Worcs/ Kidderminster	1945	IWM 3551
206	Norwich	1945	EAFA 432
210	Manchester	1945	IWM 3499
212	Manchester	1945	IWM 3500
219	Manchester	1945	IWM 3509
226	Manchester	1945	IWM 3502
241	Manchester	1946	IWM 3503
246	Manchester	1946	IWM 3504
252	Sheffield	1946	BFI
262	Sheffield	1946	BFI
266	Birkenhead	1946	IWM 7001
273	Manchester	1946	IWM 3505
285	Brighton & Hastings	1946	IWM 4967
299	Manchester	1946	IWM 3506
311	Manchester	1946	IWM 3507
328	Manchester	1946	IWM 3508
351	Dundee	1946	IWM 4786
361	Manchester	1946	IWM 3501
380	Sheffield	1946	BFI
385	Bournemouth	1946	IWM 6443
387	Sheffield	1946	BFI
388	Manchester	1946	IWM 3510

(*Continued*)

Issue	Location	Year	Film Archive/ catalogue reference
391	Brighton	1946	IWM 4968
	Glasgow	1945	IWM 2430
	Southampton	1944	Wessex FA 3629
	Northampton	1945	IWM 6703
	Newcastle (fragment)	1945	IWM 6462
	Wolverhampton	1944	BFI
	Walsall	1945	BFI
	Wigan	1945	BFI
	Bolton	1945	BFI
	York		YFA 6046
	Leeds & Doncaster		YFA 6047

TABLE C.1: IWM, Imperial War Museum; BFI, British Film Institute; MACE, Media Archive Central England; YFA, Yorkshire Film Archive; EAFA, East Anglian Film Archive.

Bibliography

Anon. (1941a), *Children Calling Home*, UK: British Pathé, https://www.britishpathe.com/video/children-calling-home/query/messages. Accessed 30 April 2019.

Anon. (1941b), *USA Sevacs tell Mum over radio*, UK: British Pathé, https://www.britishpathe.com/video/VLVA1T5R9SU182C4OMIUU79EITFR9-RELEASED-14101940/query/messages. Accessed 16 July 2020.

Anon. (1942a), *Messages Home*, Australia: Movietone.

Anon. (1942b), *The Soldier's Food*, UK: AKS.

Anon. (1943–45), *Until the Day*, UK: British Pathé, https://www.britishpathe.com/video/until-the-day. Accessed 27 July 2019.

Anon. (1944), *The Forgotten Army*, UK/Burma: British Pathé.

Anon. (1945a), *Voices of the Forces*, UK: British Pathé, https://www.britishpathe.com/video/voices-of-the-forces/query/messages). Accessed 25 April 2019.

Anon. (1945b), *Writing's worthwhile*, UK: British Pathé, https://www.britishpathe.com/video/writings-worthwhile/query/messages). Accessed 27 July 2019

Anon. (1945c), *Life in Air Command Southeast Asia*, UK: British armed forces film unit.

Anon. (1945d), *Central Front Burma*, UK: MOI.

Anstey, Edgar (1935), *Housing Problems*, UK: Realist film unit.

Asquith, Anthony (1943), *We Dive at Dawn*, UK: Gaumont British.

Atcheler, Jack (1991), audio interview by Paul Sargent, IWM.

Baskaran S. Theodore (2006), 'War Relic', *Frontline*, https://frontline.thehindu.com/arts-and-culture/cinema/article30211050.ece. Accessed 16 July 2018.

BBC Genome (2020), *Radio Times 1923–2020*, https://genome.ch.bbc.co.uk. Accessed 25 January 2020.

BBC Voices (2014), *Your voice*, http://www.bbc.co.uk/voices/yourvoice/accent2.shtml. Accessed 31 March 2019.

Bhardwaj, Vishal (2017), *Rangoon*, India: Viacom 18 Motion Pictures.

Blair, Eric (1929), 'How a nation is exploited; the British Empire in Burma', https://www.orwellfoundation.com/the-orwell-foundation/orwell/essays-and-other-works/how-a-nation-is-exploited-the-british-empire-in-burma/. Accessed 5 October 2020.

Bock, Audie (1993), *The Burmese Harp*, https://www.criterion.com/current/posts/788-the-burmese-harp. Accessed 16 June 2019.

Boulting, Roy (1946), *Burma Victory*, UK: British armed forces film units.

Brown, Tom (2012), *Breaking the Fourth Wall; Direct Address in the Cinema*, Edinburgh: Edinburgh University Press, Cited Gunning 1991: 262.

Bruch, Klaus Vom (1979), *Das Propellerband*, [video] Berlin.

Bryant, Steve (2015), 'Archive footage in new programmes: Presentational issues and perspectives', *VIEW Journal of European Television History and Culture*, 4:8, pp. 61–66.

Buchman, M. and Mussou, C. (2015), *Editorial View*, Vol 4, Issue 8, p. 1.

Bucquet, Harold, S. and Conway, Jack (1944), *Dragon Seed*, Hollywood.

Butcher, David (2016), 'Messages home: Lost films of the British army', *Radio Times*, (25 June), p. 56.

Canby, Vincent (1981), 'Let there be light; John Huston vs the Army', *New York Times,* 16 January, p. 6.

Carew, Keggie (2016), *Dadland*, London: Chatto and Windus.

Chouliaraki, Lilie (2016), 'Authoring the self: Media, voice and testimony in soldiers memoirs', *Journal of Media War and Conflict*, 9:1, pp. 58–75.

Combined Kinematograph Services (1944–46), *Calling Blighty* [series of 391 films], India/Burma.

Corner, John (1996), *The Art of Record: A Critical Introduction to Documentary*, Manchester: Manchester University Press.

Coward, Noel and Lean, David (1942), *In Which We Serve*, UK: Two Cities Films.

Crang, Jeremy A. (2000), *The British Army and the People's War, 1939–1945*, Manchester: Manchester University Press.

Das, Santanu (2020), 'India, Empire and First World War Culture', http://podcasts.ox.ac.uk/first-world-war-india-and-empire. Accessed 16 July 2019.

Dewe Mathews, Chloe (2014), *Shot At Dawn*, Tate Modern.

Dickinson, Thorold (1942), *The Next of Kin*, UK: Ealing Studios.

England, Len (2002), *Yesterday's News: The British Cinema Newsreel Reader*, London: British Universities Film & Video Council.

Fallon, Ruairi (2013), *My Father and the Forgotten Army*, BBC2, 22 May.

Farmer, Richard (2016), *Cinemas and cinemagoing in wartime Britain: The utility dream palace*, Manchester: Manchester University Press.

Fenton, James (2012), *The Forgotten Army: A Burma Soldier's Story in Letters, Photographs and Sketches*, Stroud: Fonthill.

Fiddament, Dick (1997), Audio interview by Peter Hart, IWM.

Fielding, Raymond (2011), *The American Newsreel*, Jefferson NC: McFarland & Co.

Forbes, Bryan (1965), *King Rat*, USA: Columbia Pictures.

Ford, John (1940), *The Grapes of Wrath*, USA: 20th Century Fox.

Fox, Jo. C. (2006), 'Millions like us? Accented language and the 'ordinary' in British films of the Second World War', *Journal of British studies*, 45:4, pp. 819–45.

Goodwins, Leslie (1943), *Rookies in Burma*, [film] Hollywood.

Goulty, James (2016), *The Second World War Through Soldiers' Eyes: British Army Life 1939–1945*, Barnsley: Pen & Sword Military.

Greasley, Mike (2020), e-mail to Steve Hawley, 21 October.

Guest, Val (1958), *The Camp on Blood Island*, London: Hammer Films.

Guest, Val (1959), *Yesterday's Enemy*, UK: Hammer Films.

Halbwachs, Maurice (1980), *The Collective Memory*, New York: Harper & Row.

Hawley, Steve (2016), *War Memorial*, UK: NW Film Archive.

Hawley, Steve (2019), 'War memorial: The *Calling Blighty* films and remembrance', *Media, War & Conflict*, 12:3, pp. 263–80.

Hornor, Sam (1997), audio interview by Peter Hart, IWM.

Howard, Susan (2017), interview by Rony Robinson, *Rony Robinson*, BBC Radio Sheffield, 27 March.

Huston, John (1946), *Let There Be Light*, USA: US War Department.

Ichikawa, Kon (1956), *Biruma no Tategoto [The Burmese Harp]*, Japan: Nikkatsu.

Imperial War Museum (2019), 'Terms and conditions', https://www.iwm.org.uk/sites/default/files/files/2019-10/IWM%20Terms%20and%20Conditions%20%202019.pdf. Accessed 19 June 2019.

Jackson, Pat (1944), *Western Approaches*, UK: Crown Film Unit.

Jackson, Peter (2018), *They Shall Not Grow Old*, UK: Wingnut Films.

Jarvie, Ian (1988), 'The Burma Campaign on Film', *Historical Journal of Film, Radio and Television*, 8:1, pp. 55–73.

Jenkins, Simon (2019), 'It's time to move on from these overblown commemorations of war', https://www.theguardian.com/commentisfree/2019/jun/06/commemorations-war-d-day-europe. Accessed 13 June 2019.

Jennings, Humphrey (1941), *The Heart of Britain*, UK: MOI.

Jennings, Humphrey (1943), *Fires Were Started*, UK: Crown Film Unit.

Jennings, Humphrey and McAllister, Stuart (1942), *Listen To Britain*, UK: Crown Film Unit.

Kelly, Gene and Donen, Stanley (1952), *Singing in the rain*, USA: MGM.

Khan, Yasmin (2015), *The Raj at War: A People's History of India's Second World War*, London: The Bodley Head.

Klein, Kerwin L. (2000), 'On the emergence of memory in historical discourse', *Representations*, 69 (Winter), p. 127.

Langley, Brian (2003), 'The AKS', *The Veteran*, 98, pp. 12–16.

Launder, Frank and Gilliatt, Sydney (1943), *Millions Like Us*, UK: Gainsborough Studios.

Lean, David (1957), *The Bridge over the River Kwai*, USA: Horizon Pictures.

Lee, Norman (1934), *The Forgotten men*, UK: Jewell Productions.

Lee, Jack (1941), *Ordinary People*, UK: Crown Film Unit.

LeRoy, Mervyn (1944), *Thirty Seconds Over Tokyo*, USA: MGM.

Lewis, Joseph H. (1942), *Bombs Over Burma*, USA: Producers Releasing Corporation.

Lewis, Alun (1989), *Letters to My Wife*, Bridgend: Seren Books.

Losh, Jack (2019), 'Africans who fought for British army paid less than white soldiers', *The Guardian*, 13 February, https://www.theguardian.com/world/2019/feb/13/african-british-army-paid-less-than-white-soldiers. Accessed 28 June 2019.

Mackay, Robert (2003), *Half the Battle: Civilian Morale in Britain During the Second World War*, Manchester: Manchester University Press.

Mackenzie, S. P. (2001), *British War Films 1939–1945*, London: Hambledon and London.

Macrae, Ben (1997), audio interview by Peter Hart, IWM.

Mantel, Hilary (2017), 'Hilary Mantel: Why I became a historical novelist', *The Guardian*, 3 June.

March, Winsome (2017), 'Interview by Rony Robinson', *Rony Robinson*, BBC Radio Sheffield, 27 March.

Mark, Joshua J. (2017), 'Thutmose III's Battle of Megiddo Inscription', https://www.ancient.eu/article/1102/thutmose-iiis-battle-of-megiddo-inscription/. Accessed 23 December 2019.

Mason, A. and Parton, E. (2018), 'Letters to loved ones', https://www.iwm.org.uk/history/letters-to-loved-ones. Accessed 20 June 2019.

McCormack, Stephen (1943), personal diary, 28 December.

McKernan, Luke (2019), 'Messages from the Army in Italy (1944)', https://lukemckernan.com/2019/06/26/filming-windrush/. Accessed 21 May 2019.

McLynn, Frank (2011), *The Burma Campaign Disaster into Triumph 1942–1945*, London: Vintage.

Memorial Gates (2019), 'Campaigns, Burma and India', https://memorialgates.org/history/ww2/campaigns/burma-india.html. Accessed 20 June 2019.

Messages Home: Lost Films of the British Army (2016), [TV programme]: Channel 4.

Metcalfe, Nick (2016), 'Burma's secret jungle war with Joe Simpson', [online], BBC2, https://www.bbc.co.uk/iplayer/episode/b07c9rz9/burmas-secret-jungle-war-with-joe-simpson-episode-2. Accessed 20 July 2020.

Milward, Alan (2000), 'Bad Memories', *The Times Literary Supplement*, 14 April 2000, p. 8.

Munden, Max (1941), *Shunter Black's Night Off*, UK: MOI.

Myint-U, Thant (2008), 'The shared history of Britain and Burma', *Daily Telegraph*, 11 May, n.pag.

National Science and Media Museum (2011), 'A Short History of British television', https://blog.scienceandmediamuseum.org.uk/history-of-british-television-timeline/. Accessed 2 May 2019.

Norman, Leslie (1961), *The Long and the Short and the Tall*, UK: Michael Balcon Productions, ABPC.

Osborne, Richard (2009), 'Colonial film Burma Victory', https://film.iwmcollections.org.uk/record/637. Accessed 21 March 2019.

Osborne, Richard (2010), 'Life in air command south-east Asia', http://www.colonialfilm.org.uk/node/5430. Accessed 20 February 2020.

Osborne, Richard (2010), 'The Stillwell Road', http://www.colonialfilm.org.uk/node/6679. Accessed 4 Feb 2019.

Ōshima, Nagisa (1983), *Merry Christmas Mr Lawrence*, Japan: Oshime Productions.

Our special correspondent (1944), 'Army talkie "brings back" soldiers to their families', *News Chronicle*, p. 3.

Our special correspondent (1944), 'Army talkie brings back soldiers to their families', *News Chronicle*, 4 February, p. 2.

Our special correspondent (1945), 'British answer to Objective Burma', *Aberdeen Press and Journal*, 26 September, p. 8.

Oxford English Dictionary (2017), 'In: 1st ed', http://www.oed.com.ezproxy.mmu.ac.uk. Accessed 21 June 2016.

Parr, E. (1945), 'A Soldier writes from Malaya', *Worthing Herald*, 26 October, p. 11.

Porter, Dennis (2016), audio interview by Steve Hawley.

Presnell, Robert (1945), *The Stilwell Road*, USA: Office of War Information.

Rattigan, Neil (2001), *This is England: British Film and the people's war 1939–45*, Ontario: Fairleigh Dickinson University Press.

Reed, Carol (1944), *The Way Ahead*, UK: Two Cities Films.

Reisz, Karel (1959), *We Are The Lambeth Boys*, UK: Ford Motor Company.

Richards, Jeffrey and Sheridan, Dorothy (1987), *Mass Observation at the Movies*, London: Routledge and Kegan Paul.

Rieff, David (2016), 'The cult of memory: when history does more harm than good', *The Guardian*, 2 March, https://www.theguardian.com/education/2016/mar/02/cult-of-memory-when-history-does-more-harm-than-good. Accessed 18 September 2019.

Rothwell, Steve (2016), *The Forgotten Army* (press release).

Ruth-Rice, David (2014), 'This 1800 year old letter is from a homesick soldier', https://www.futurity.org/ancient-letter-shows-soldiers-longing-home/. Accessed 2 February 2019.

Salerno, Shane and Shields, David (2013), *Salinger*, New York: Simon & Schuster.

Sargent, Paul (1992), 'Keep smiling, keep those chins up and God bless: Filmed messages home from service personnel in the Far East during the Second World War', *Imperial War Museum Review*, 7, pp. 23–33.

Sherman, Vincent (1949), *The Hasty Heart*, USA: Warner Brothers.

Sylvan, Simon S. (1942), *The Grand Central Murder*, USA: MGM.

Slim, William (1956), *Defeat into Victory*, London: Cassell.

Smith, Adrian (2003), 'Humphrey Jennings Heart of Britain (1941): A reassessment', *Historical Journal of Film, Radio and Television*, 23:2, pp. 133–51.

Sparrow, Col J. H. A, (1949), 'The Second World War 1939–1943', *Army Morale*, War Office, p. 9.

Spicer, Andrew (2003), 'Extending people's minds for a brief time every day: The wartime propaganda short', *Journal of Media Practice*, 4:2, pp. 105–12.

Spiers Edward, M. (2018), 'The Victorian soldier in Africa', https://www.manchesteropenhive.com/view/9781526137913/9781526137913.00008.xml. Accessed 20th July 2019

Sundaram, Tiruchengodu. R. (1945), *Burma Rani*, India: Modern Theatres.

Sussex, Elizabeth (1975), *The Rise and Fall of British Documentary*, Berkley: University of California Press.

Tewson, Miles (2016), *The Process of Decolonization in Burma: Managing the Transition from Colony to Independent State* [Honours Dissertation], pp. 16–30. https://www.northumbria.ac.uk/media/25804399/miles-tewson.pdf. Accessed 16 July 2019.

Thapa, Narain (2004), *The Boy from Lambata: Memoirs of a Combat Cameraman and Documentary-maker*, India: Peoples Association for Himalaya Area Research.

The Screen New York Times (1945), 'Objective, Burma, a realistic and excitingly told war film starring Errol Flynn', https://www.nytimes.com/1945/01/27/archives/the-screen-objective-burma-a-realistic-and-excitingly-told-war-film.html. Accessed 15 March 2019.

Thumim, Nancy (2012), *Self-Representation and Digital Culture*, London: Palgrave Macmillan.

Timeline of the BBC (2020), 'Timeline of the BBC', https://en.wikipedia.org/wiki/Timeline_of_the_BBC. Accessed 20 June 2019.

Varnel, Marcel (1940), *Let George Do It*, UK: Ealing Studios.

Walker, Alexander (2005), *Hollywood England: The British Film Industry in the 1960s*, London: Orion Publishing.

Walker, Rob (2018), audio interview by Steve Hawley.

Walsh, Raoul (1945), *Objective, Burma*: USA: Warner Brothers.

Watt, Harry (1941), *Target For Tonight*, UK: MOI.

Wikipedia (2010), 'Alun Lewis (poet)', https://en.wikipedia.org/wiki/Alun_Lewis_(poet). Accessed 25 November 2019.

Wikipedia (2020), 'Ngoma Drums', https://en.wikipedia.org/wiki/Ngoma_drums. Accessed 13 July 2019.

Williams, Tennessee (1944), 'The Glass Menagerie', https://www.brainyquote.com/quotes/tennessee_williams_147304. Accessed 25 January 2019.

Winter, Jay (2017), *War beyond Words: Languages of Remembrance from the Great War to the Present,* Yale University, Connecticut: Cambridge University Press.

Winter, Jay M. (2006), *Remembering War: The Great War Between Memory and History in the Twentieth Century*, Yale: Yale University Press.

Winter, J. and Sivan, E. (eds) (1999), *War and Remembrance in the Twentieth Century*, Cambridge: Cambridge University Press.

Winterson, Jeanette (2012), *Why Be Happy When You Could Be Normal?*, London: Vintage.

Woolcock, Penny (2013), *From the sea to the land and beyond*, UK: Crossover.

Ww2today.com (2016), 'Britain's Longest campaign of Word War 2 – Burma', [online], http://ww2today.com/featured/burma-britains-longest-campaign-of-world-war-ii. Accessed 20 April 2016.

Wyler, William (1942), *Mrs Miniver*, USA: MGM.

Young, Rob (2010), *Electric Eden*, London: Faber and Faber.

Index

Lightning Source UK Ltd.
Milton Keynes UK
UKHW031757011022
409727UK00001B/32